BUSINESS TRANSFORMATION: A PATH TO PROFITABILITY FOR THE MAILING & FULFILLMENT INDUSTRIES

BUSINESS TRANSFORMATION: A PATH TO PROFITABILITY FOR THE MAILING & FULFILLMENT INDUSTRIES

By: John P. Foley, Jr.

ISBN 978-0-615-59995-3

"Business Transformation starts with planning and change. Maximize the success of your transformation by spending time on the strategies before applying the tactics."

ACKNOWLEDGEMENTS

I would like to consider this book a culmination of my experience in business and marketing throughout my career. It would not be possible without the continuous love and support from my mother and father. Thank you for shaping me into the person who I am today and always pushing me to go after my dreams. I also wish to thank my beautiful wife, Melanie, for her unconditional support in all aspects of my life. To my 3 boys, Matt, Trevor, and Luke, thanks for your time and patience along the way. Remember to "follow your dreams" - I love you all! Dad

I also wish to thank my dedicated staff for making all of this possible. I appreciate all of your hard work. Finally, a thank you to Cary Sherburne for helping me to write this book with the utmost forbearance.

How to Connect

Thank you very much for taking the time to read this book. If you have some free time, I'd love to chat with you. If you have any thoughts about business transformation, the mailing & fulfillment industries, multi-channel marketing, this book or anything else, feel free to send me a note. You can reach me on Twitter at http:// Twitter.com/JohnFoleyJr.

Mobilized Page created by http://www.iFlyMobi.com

FOREWORD

By: Ken Garner

Without periodic modification even the most successful business models fail over time. This is particularly true of businesses trapped in over-populated, mature industries where commoditization has eroded margins necessary for business survival. If you can't effectively differentiate your service offering and sell on the basis of value instead of price, you can't succeed. Sound familiar?

This is an unfortunate reality for many, if not most, mailing service providers who are painfully slugging it out in today's hyper-competitive market space. An uncertain future for the USPS only adds uncertainty and anxiety. And, while many fulfillment service providers are enjoying better times, they understand that long-term success depends on an on-going review of the strength of their business models and value propositions in order to avoid a sales stall point.

Breaking away from equipment based transactional customer relationships requires more than courage. A successful transformation requires careful planning and execution. You need a road map that provides specific step-by-step guidance to help you successfully navigate a tricky competitive landscape. Fortunately, with ***Business Transformation: A Path to Profitability for the Mailing and Fulfillment Industries***, John Foley provides a comprehensive and definitive transformation guide for those who desire to move to a more profitable and sustainable competitive position. A teacher at heart, John has demonstrated a passion for sharing the benefit of his considerable experience and expertise. You won't find any vague, overly-academic theory here. He delivers practical guidance based on his experience as an entrepreneur and successful marketer.

John effectively lays out all of the critical elements required for a successful transition to becoming a marketing services provider. He carefully leads you through the critically important planning process and ends with what you need to do to effectively market and promote your new enterprise. He even provides templates and forms to simplify your process. Perhaps best of all are the numerous case studies that provide real-world examples of successful transformations.

No more excuses. This book provides both the catalyst for action as well as the guidance necessary to successfully complete the task that moves you and your company to a more sustainable competitive advantage.

TABLE OF CONTENTS

TABLE OF FIGURES

Access to Additional Resources

In the true spirit of a digital world, this book is supported by an online resources portal that will provide additional tools and resources as well as new content as it becomes available. We believe that will make this book even more valuable, and we encourage you to take advantage of these resources.

Throughout the book, we have included QR Codes such as the one below that will take you to related portal content.

Using a smart phone equipped with a QR Code reader application, simply point at the QR Code to access the portal, or type the URL below the code into your browser.

**To access the portal,
scan the QR Code above,
or type
http://www.NewPathToProfit.com
into your computer's web browser**

QR Codes are 2-dimensional barcodes that make print interactive. To scan them, you need a smart phone, such as an iPhone, Android-based phone or Blackberry, and a QR Code-reader app. The apps are typically free and easy to access.

Visit http://QReateAndTrack.com for a list of reader applications for different phones.

CHAPTER ONE

INTRODUCTION

Marketing Communications: From the Kitchen Table to Your Bottom-Line

If ever there were industries in need of transformation, it is the mailing & fulfillment industries. As we enter the second decade of the century, this mature industry is consolidating faster than anyone ever expected, and postal volumes are experiencing steep declines. In fact, according to Dr. Joe Webb, Director of the Economics & Research Center for online media company WhatTheyThink[1], the number of First Class mail pieces declined 31.8% between 2000 and 2010. Standard Mail, the USPS designation for discounted high-volume mail that meets USPS guidelines for sorting and postal automation, declined by 13.7%, and periodical pieces declined a whopping 35.1%. It is no secret that the USPS is struggling, and this decline in mail volume doesn't help either the post office or its mailing customers.

Mail isn't going away, but it isn't what it used to be—the primary method of getting information to consumers and businesses. There are two ways that we can interpret this – first, in terms of the declining volume of mail, and secondly, by observing what happens in my kitchen.

The Kitchen Table Effect: Understanding Generational Differences

Let me begin by telling you how my family communicates and consumes information today in the kitchen.

My two teenage boys hardly ever pick up a printed copy of a magazine. They do occasionally, but only if the front cover is personalized with their name, or maybe if their name is on the back of a hockey jersey on the back cover, or something to that effect. My youngest son (Luke) prefers to communicate and get information via Facebook and the Internet. My middle son (Trevor) uses Facebook but is not addicted. He prefers to communicate via text messaging. Matthew, my oldest, loves his smart phone and does everything with it – Do I need to repeat "Everything"? He is religious about checking his various social media venues via phone and texting, keeping up with the news and more.

The point is that their generation uses different communications channels than we grew up with. And I know a lot of folks that struggle with some of these forms of communication. I have heard it all—"It is

---

[1] http://members.whattheythink.com/erc/erc.cfm (most content is free).

impersonal; they won't know how to speak properly; they won't be social."

What? They won't be social? Some of today's channels allow them to be more social than ever! It is just hard for some people to understand—change can be difficult.

Finally, if businesses want to reach my boys, they must recognize this change in how younger folks communicate—and how they want to be communicated with. Simply pushing printed materials to them through the mail will not work anymore, I'm sorry to say. Mail is NOT going away, but its role in today's communications certainly has changed.

Consider this: There are three primary generations sharing the workplace today: Baby Boomers, Gen X'ers and Gen Y. Gen Y, or Generation Y, also known as the Millennial Generation, refers to the generation with birth dates somewhere from the mid-1970s to the early 2000s, according to www.wikipedia.org. Sixty million people in the U.S. were born after the Internet went into public use in 1995, marked by Netscape's IPO. According to WhatTheyThink's Webb, demographics data indicate that the U.S. population will have 110 million new people immersed in digital communications by 2020, with 30 million of those with generally low digital media use having "exited" the marketplace.

When I think about multi-channel marketing, I think about how my own family uses communications tools differently. I also think about how receptive they would be to various communication methods. This includes my three boys, ages 15 (Luke), 17 (Trevor), and 24 (Matthew)[2], and my beautiful wife (Melanie). My 15-year-old is a dedicated Facebooker and a big-time texter. He can bang out more text in a fast and furious way than you could ever think possible and he thinks nothing of it. As for his Facebooking, he checks it in the AM, after school, and before bed. My 17-year-old checks his stuff on his phone and may post a picture here or there but doesn't communicate all the time in that channel like his younger brother does. However, he does text, not at the speed or as often as his brother does, but he does use it. They both watch Sports Center (TV) religiously every day, but I never see the older of the two grab the hockey magazine. However, my youngest son will. My oldest son, well, he Facebooks and text-messages a little, and he also uses the phone, surfs the web, and checks

---

[2] Ages as of 2010

sports scores. One thing is for sure, they will all respond rapidly to a text message. Many times, you will make a phone call and will get a text answer back in seconds. Don't bother leaving a voice mail—none of them even listen to those! The point is, like it or not, this is the way they communicate. Lots of folks struggle with this communication methodology because they feel it is impersonal; however, I disagree. Some of these channels, like texting, are immediate, can be to the point, and the communication can be effective.

Melanie and I text, phone, and still get the postal mail. I admit, when I get the mail, it's usually one for me and one for the recycle bin. I'm the only one that is fond of direct marketers who spend time personalizing marketing pieces or getting creative (and I'm not talking about simply including my first and last name). But maybe that is because of the business I am in. As for Melanie, not so much.

Also, we hardly receive any bills via mail anymore because we have opted to go paperless, receiving email notifications and paying them online, and most of them with automatic payments. Our home phone is rarely used. If we are all in the kitchen and the phone rings, we all look at each other, and no one goes for the phone. We all just start laughing, as no one will pick it up. No one calls any of us on that number, except for sales calls, or maybe automated messages that we can check voicemail for later. We constantly have the discussion around the house as to whether or not we even still need a landline.

The day I was writing this, the landline phone rang, and I actually answered it. It was one of our friends. She said, "I didn't think you were ever going to answer." I said, "Well, Donna, I almost didn't, but saw it was a local number. By the way, you are the first friend of ours to call us on this line in years. Did you lose your cell phone?" She laughed and said, "No, I left it in the car and thought I would use the old-fashioned phone." The point is, for our family, the telemarketing to our landline is "Dead on Arrival (DOA)," much like many marketing communications methods today for some targeted demographics, including direct mail.

Wait, what about my 82-year-old dad? The phone still works but you had better be prepared to use a loud voice and hold the earpiece away from your head as he responds! And forget the Personalized URL for him; it won't work. He prefers traditional marketing. Oh, and he still buys things! He still loves his mail and the newspaper. The reason I point this out is that it very important to understand the consumer's behavior and the ways each consumes information and participates in marketing communications. For you, the marketing services provider, it is equally important that you, as someone trying to reach each target demographic, understand how they participate and communicate. There is not a single silver bullet for all, and there really has never been, although it seemed that marketing worked that way in the past.

The State of the Mailing Industry

So back to the sad state of mail:

It is no secret that the United States Postal Service (USPS) is facing a dire situation. One could argue that many its woes link back to a single date in history: August 9, 1995. That was the date Netscape went public. *Fortune Magazine*[3] called it "the spark that touched off the Internet boom." Demand for the shares was so high that trading couldn't open for nearly two hours. The stock was priced at $28, hit a high of $75, and closed that day at $58.

Sure, the Internet had been around for some time before that, but Netscape captured the imagination of consumers and the business world and marked the beginning of what has become known as the "dot-com" boom. The *Fortune* story continues, "Until then, Silicon Valley was just a place where microchips were made, not the fountainhead of global commerce. The public was oblivious to the Internet; 'surfing' meant catching a wave in the ocean or mindlessly flicking the TV's remote control."

In the early days of the Internet boom, many mailing & fulfillment companies benefited from the wild spending sprees of the dot-com companies who, among other things, used printed materials to promote their businesses and needed mailing and fulfillment services to get them into the marketplace. Perhaps owners of mailing & fulfillment businesses were too caught up in this "pot of gold" to take the time to understand what was happening. Regardless, many continued "business as usual" until September 11, 2001, when many things social and economic came to a screeching halt—including print purchases, and the mailing and fulfillment activities that went along with them. Yet direct mail volumes continued to grow. According to the USPS Household Diary Study, 2010, in 1987, the average U.S.

---

[3] "Remembering Netscape: The Birth of the Web," by Adam Lashinsky, *Fortune Magazine,* July 25, 2005.

household received 7.8 pieces of standard mail per week, including catalogs. By 2008, that number rose to 11.4, largely due to the high volumes of mail from the financial services industry.

But things were about to change dramatically as the housing market in the U.S. began to crumble and the subprime mortgage crisis caused a global recession, with its roots in the announcement by the Federal Home Loan Mortgage Corporation (Freddie Mac) in February of 2007 that it would no longer buy the most risky subprime mortgages and mortgage-related securities.[4] As the financial crisis began to take hold, the number dropped to 9.5 pieces of mail received by the average U.S. household by 2009.

While the deep global recession didn't officially start, at least from a U.S. perspective, until December of 2007, as stated by the National Bureau of Economic Research in December 2008 (amazing how economic data lags in getting analyzed and to the market!), the writing was on the Facebook wall for the printing, mailing and fulfillment industries, for those who cared to read it.

This recession was totally different. It was not one that could be "waited out for a return to business as usual," as had been the case in the past. There were a vast array of alternatives to printed communications being rapidly adopted. Total annual USPS mail volumes went from a high of 213 billion pieces in 2006 to 169 billion in 2010, a drop of 21%. Meanwhile, the percent of that total represented by advertising mail continued to grow, from 49.6% in 2006, to 53.3% in 2010.

With the volume of First Class mail—the most profitable component for the USPS—falling, and standard mail starting to decline as well, some industry pundits wonder whether the USPS will implode, or will actually be able to reinvent itself under the new leadership of Postmaster General Patrick Donahoe as services in many other countries have. *Bloomberg Business Week* published an article in 2011 that presented a very gloomy picture of the future of this organization (http://goo.gl/byENK).

And as marketers and other decision-makers turned increasingly to digital channels, perceived as less expensive, and more effective than printed mail, there was not much likelihood that they would ever

---

[4] *The Financial Crisis: A Timeline of Events and Policy Actions*, Federal Reserve Bank of St. Louis, http://timeline.stlouisfed.org/index.cfm?p=timeline

revert to using printed mail in the same way once a recovery was underway. Later in the game, as businesses realized that some of these digital channels were easier to measure than traditional channels, it further pushed them to make a shift.

This look back at history is important in understanding how deeply this mature and consolidating industry has been affected by all of these factors. The industry will continue to be negatively affected in the future unless businesses take the steps necessary to transform themselves to meet the needs of the new market realities. In fact, Eric Liggett, General Manager of Kent Communications, who provided a case study for this book, went so far as to say, "Some [firms] are getting around this by partnering with mailing houses that don't print. But I believe that is a dying breed that won't be around in another five years or so." Steve Smits of vision Integrated Graphics, another case study included in this book, added, "At some point in time, there will still be the huge printers and the huge mailers, but below that it will be a blended business model."

A positive factor within this overall gloom that direct mail providers often fail to consider lies with the fact that the more difficult the USPS becomes to deal with, as it undergoes cuts in employment, facilities and more, the more direct mailers will have to rely on the skills of the suppliers they use. Mailing and fulfillment firms that have developed not only a good understanding of changing postal regulations, but also have developed good relationships with USPS supervisors at mail acceptance facilities, can position this knowledge and these relationships as a competitive advantage to their customers as they look for partners willing to directly manage the mailing process.

Another factor that is beginning to negatively impact mail volumes arises due to the fact that the USPS has no digital strategy. New services are arising to fill that vacuum, such as Zumbox and the Pitney Bowes Volly initiative as well as others.[5] The aim of these services is to take even more mail out of the mailstream, starting with transactional mail, but quickly moving into the advertising mail space. To do so, these services are partnering with large transactional service

---

[5] Volly, Zumbox and others are digital mailbox solutions that allow large transactional printers and direct mailers to deliver transactional, advertising and other types of mail directly to a secure digital mailbox without the need to print and mail these documents.

bureaus, such as DST Output, that produce billions of mail pieces each year, as well as providing options for smaller mailers to participate. These private digital mailbox services allow companies such as DST Output to offer their customers an easy, affordable and secure digital alternative to placing customer communications in the mail stream. While it is anticipated, even by the vendors providing these services, that it will take some time for these services to become mainstream, they ultimately will have an effect on mail volumes. The exact timing of that impact is unclear.

Trends and Opportunities in Fulfillment

If the Internet made life difficult for print and mail, it opened up new opportunities in fulfillment, especially as ecommerce began to take off and web storefronts peddled all types of products, including print. While fulfillment services had been limited to physical items in the warehouse, fulfillment of electronic materials, ranging from transactional documents to PDFs of brochures, was now gaining steam. Opportunities for growth lay with those that could bridge the gap between physical and digital materials.

Clearly, the growth of ecommerce also provided significant growth in the area of product fulfillment as consumers and businesses alike began purchasing more via the web. Additionally, the growing functionality of web storefronts opened yet another door for those willing to invest in new infrastructure: the ability to source materials from multiple manufacturers through a single, seamless storefront experience. Amazon.com, of course, was the guiding light for this business model. But increasingly, fulfillment businesses are offering these value-added services.

There are other value-added services that can be included in a full-service offering that raises fulfillment services beyond the commodity zone. This allows fulfillment services business to integrate with lead generation programs, fielding calls and fulfilling all requested materials, whether printed, promotional, warehoused products, apparel or digital materials. From that point, it is a relatively simple leap to begin executing and managing lead generation programs on behalf of the client—morphing what could be considered a commodity fulfillment operation into a true marketing services offering.

Finally, with the advanced capabilities and ease of use in today's digital printing presses (including digital offset or DI presses), it is easier than ever before for mailing & fulfillment businesses to introduce printing into the mix. This allows them to serve customers with a print-on-demand model, eliminating many of the costs incurred due to inventory management and obsolescence of printed materials. It also makes it easier to combine mailings or shipments comprised of printed and non-printed materials, generating or storing all or most required components under one roof.

Avoiding the Mistakes of the Past

Geoffrey Moore's book, *Crossing the Chasm,* which I read many years ago, is about technology companies making the jump with new products or services over the "chasm." It defined early adopters and innovators, describing how they react and move through a dynamically changing environment in a different manner than mainstream adopters. The book also explains what happens if you are late to the game. There is clearly a correlation between a technology company moving through the winding road to success without dropping into the chasm (as many have) and today's mailing & fulfillment company that is working to transform itself with new business offerings and a new approach to customers.

I have been in business long enough to have seen companies continually repeat the mistakes of the past while trying to move forward. Business transformation in any industry presents significant challenges. But with a good strategy and a proven path to follow, companies can grow and profit. This book is about helping you make that transformation, "jumping" as quickly and easily as possible over the chasm, while remaining viable and profitable. It lays out a set of strategies that can be adapted to almost any company in the mailing & fulfillment industries, strategies that are built on studies of those that have been adopted by companies who are successfully transforming themselves, or have already transformed themselves, and are reaping the benefits.

This Business Transformation book was born from years of watching mailing & fulfillment companies struggle with the concept of delivering marketing services to boost their portfolio of offerings in response to changing market demand, and then further struggling to implement the disciplines and resources required to execute the new strategies. Some are succeeding, but others continue to throw one dart at a time at the board and wonder why it is not working. Or worse yet, others just stare at the dart board and wonder where the darts are.

I am almost fanatically convinced, based on my experience in the marketplace, that there are clear paths to transformation for any mailing & fulfillment company with the will to make the effort. This book not only lays out those paths and strategies, but includes tools such as business plan and marketing plan templates and more, to make the path easier to follow. It is a handbook for mailing & fulfillment businesses who want to move into the future as marketing automation service providers, or whatever other nomenclature they want to use in describing their businesses. It is a more customer-centric approach that asks, "What keeps you awake at night and how can we help you with those issues?"

Not every business will or should convert. There will be a need in the foreseeable future for companies who can deliver commodity mailing & fulfillment services associated with direct mail campaigns, product and literature fulfillment and the like. But those companies are likely to be fighting it out with companies like those profiled in this book, winning only by taking margins almost to the breaking point. Alternatively, we have seen that companies who have transformed their businesses to meet these new market realities are growing and profitable, even during tough economic times, and finding ways around the price erosion surrounding commodity mailing services. This book includes some of their stories, in which they frankly share what worked, what didn't, and how their overall business was affected.

Web-Based Marketing a Central Theme

I came to the industry with a business background, strong in marketing. I had an idea in 1996 that I could create a web-based marketing solution that would allow enterprises and eventually mailing & fulfillment operations, to grow their businesses by offering more marketing-oriented services to their clients. Remember, this was just one year after the Netscape IPO, and most in the mailing & fulfillment industries were hard-pressed to see what was coming at them. Now, I don't have a crystal ball, nor could I possibly have envisioned back then the ultimate outcome for the industry. But I knew I was on to something big. Perhaps we were ahead of our time. Despite the many rejections in those early years, we kept on keeping on, and the persistence is paying off more than a decade later with a growing number of companies that understand not only that the transformation is critical, but are willing to stick their toe in the water and get started. Some use products from my company, interlinkONE; some use products from other companies or homegrown systems. But I like to think that our early efforts were a catalyst in getting this movement going and salvaging at least some subset of a venerable industry whose indicators are going in the wrong direction.

What You Will Learn

In Chapter Two, we take a deeper look at the driving forces behind the need for business transformation in the mailing & fulfillment industries, as well as the usual objections we run into when people believe they can continue with "business as usual." We poke some holes in that thought process and back that up with research demonstrating what marketers are seeking from their service provider partners. We also delve into what it really means to be a marketing services provider, and use real-world examples of companies that have transformed—or are in the process of transforming—their businesses. It's not a one-size-fits-all, but any company can get some great ideas from these examples. We posit that it doesn't really matter what you call yourself—we use the term "marketing services provider" throughout the book as a convenience. But tagging your company with a new moniker is often an important part of the repositioning effort.

Chapter Three dives deeper into what it means to be a marketing services provider. Some of the important questions we address include: How do you manage the development of new business while still protecting the legacy business and allowing it to fund new development and innovation? How quickly should you expect this transformation to occur? How do you balance short transactional sales cycles with the long sales cycles generally associated with the delivery of marketing services and other types of solution selling?

Chapter Four is really the heart of the book. It provides a detailed look at how to build and execute against business and marketing plans. Examples are available in this chapter and in the appendices. Templates are available on a special online resource page we have set up especially for readers of this book.

In Chapter Five, we move on to infrastructure considerations— people, processes and technology that will be required as you transform your business. Don't worry—we don't get too geeky and technical here. The discussions are more business-oriented. This is also an important element of the book. Becoming a marketing services provider is more complex than installing a new inserter. It touches every aspect of your organization and requires new skills that you must bring in house or find through partners.

With your business and marketing plans in hand and your infrastructure under control, turn to Chapter Six. It offers tips and guidance on being the best-ever marketing services provider. In Chapter Seven, we take it a step further with a deep dive into how you should be promoting your new business. That naturally takes us to the next step: the selling process, covered in Chapter Eight. As you will see, selling marketing services requires a totally different approach than traditionally used in selling mailing & fulfillment services. This may also require seeking new talent, oftentimes from outside the industry.

Chapter Nine is one of my favorites, and the topic is on-line marketing to include social media. While anything written on this topic is obsolete almost as fast as it is written in this quickly-evolving space, Chapter Nine contains good background on key social media sites as well as specific guidelines about how to use them and stay current.

Chapter Ten wraps up our time together in this book with a summary and some next steps. But wait! There is more! Don't forget to join us at http://www.NewPathToProfit.com where you will find lots of tips, tools, updates and the opportunity to discuss this transformation process with your peers. Of course, we have added many appendices to the book as well, to provide you as many tools in one package as possible. But the resource page will also include Excel spreadsheets, business and marketing plan templates, live self-promotional examples and much, much more that I hope will speed your transformation along. There are a number of success cases out there, as you will see in this book. Why reinvent the wheel? There is much to be learned from those who have gone before you.

My goal is that this book will bring you some hope about the future and some new directions in which you can take your business. If you have already started the transformation, or even completed it, there are still valuable lessons shared in this book that can benefit your business, as well as tools and strategies you may wish to adopt as you continue your journey.

CHAPTER TWO

PATIENCE, PERSEVERANCE AND PERSPECTIVE

From Rome to Route 128: Learning from Leaders in the Industry

Transforming a business is never easy. Whether it is a software business such as the one I run or a mailing & fulfillment business seeking to add products and services that meet new and different customer needs, there are many challenges to be faced. But it can be done, and it has been done by many companies. Transformation takes patience, perseverance and perspective, especially when introducing breakthrough offerings that are perhaps unexpected and ahead of their time in terms of mainstream market acceptance.

When I first began calling on printers and mailing & fulfillment companies in the mid-1990s, I was offering a software solution that enabled them to deliver integrated multichannel marketing solutions. I suggested that there was an opportunity for them in offering more marketing-oriented services, and that I had a solution that could help them do so. That terminology and those ideas were much more foreign a decade ago than they are today. Perhaps not surprisingly, I got a number of reactions, none of which made me particularly happy or boded well for closing sales. These included:

- I'm a mailer. I don't offer marketing services.
- I deal in hard goods. There is no way for me to make money on electronic services.
- You don't understand my business.
- We warehouse things and ship them out the door. Why would I want to get into email marketing?
- And my favorite: The Internet is a fad—this from a fulfillment company that was well-known at the time.

It was not easy being thrown out the door time after time, but my team and I kept at it with patience and perseverance. I tried to keep a positive perspective, understanding that this transformation was a breakthrough idea and there would be many who would not understand. Oddly enough, we had some success in offering these solutions to enterprise customers—the customers of the printers, and mailing & fulfillment houses—who could see the value to their businesses. Had printers, mailers and fulfillment houses been offering these services, those enterprises may well have purchased them from the service provider instead of directly from my company. We strongly believed that mailing & fulfillment operations needed to diversify their businesses in order to stay competitive and profitable. In addition, these service providers would become a sales channel to the enterprise for us. So we kept at it. We did not allow the negativity of naysayers to discourage us from continuing to build an offering that would allow a service provider to become a more valuable part of the enterprise marketing organization. We continued to try to educate the market about the value of moving up the marketing supply chain, locking customers into long-term annuity business relationships that delivered new revenue streams for their businesses and new levels of productivity for them and their customers.

Trade show after trade show, "kicking the tires" executives would come to our booth and ask what we did. For many, it did not take long for their eyes to glaze over and for them to obviously begin seeking an escape from the discussion. It took a decade before we started seeing mailing & fulfillment professionals showing up in any meaningful numbers at our trade show booth or calling our offices saying, "I have a general understanding of why I should be offering integrated marketing services. Show me why I should use your solution." These were knowledgeable and informed business owners who knew what they needed to do for their businesses and were sincerely seeking the best match. What a breakthrough! Many of these early adopters and innovators became our customers, and we are proud of the fact that we are able to continue to help them grow, supporting them with new ideas and solutions.

Today, we are successfully offering these web-based solutions to printers as well as mailing & fulfillment providers that enable their customers to build, manage, execute and measure their multichannel marketing efforts. This success is largely due to our patience and perseverance, and to not losing perspective. We had a vision and we kept working toward it, despite many setbacks.

That's our story in a nutshell. We were able to build a successful company serving a market need that we could clearly see, but that many in the industry we were trying to serve could not fathom at the time. That's not much different, really, than the challenge facing mailing & fulfillment businesses as they reposition themselves to provide leading-edge solutions to *their* customers. The rest of this book is devoted to helping make this necessary business transformation easier for mailing & fulfillment businesses who have not yet taken the plunge, or for accelerating and expanding the transformation for those who have begun.

One other thing to keep in mind as you read this book: This is not installing a new inserter or adding robotic warehouse equipment.

Those are projects with a beginning and an end in terms of implementation. You buy the gear, you work through the bumps of integrating it into your workflow, and you start producing and keep on producing. That is not business transformation; it is merely upgrading existing services using newer and better technology. The type of transformation we are speaking about here—adding integrated marketing-oriented services to the mix—does not negate the need to keep other technology up to date. But what it does imply is the beginning of a journey without an end, but with many rewards along the way.

By now, everyone in the mailing & fulfillment industries knows, or should know, that the Internet is not a fad. They know that the mailing business is in the midst of extreme structural change that requires them to change their approach to the market—or if they don't, they certainly should as they look at their P&L each month. They know that much of the printed materials their customers used to send to them for mailing and/or fulfillment doesn't even get printed anymore, or if it does, the run lengths get shorter and shorter and the delivery times continue to compress, making it more attractive for printers to do the fulfillment themselves rather than outsource to a third party. And they should understand that if they don't have the right infrastructure in place to accommodate emerging customer needs, they risk not only declining business from good, long-term customers, but losing them altogether. We see this being played out in the marketplace every single day.

There Are No Guarantees in Life

Business transformation is not for everyone, and there are no guarantees that simply heading down the path will lead to future success. Nor does adding the tag "marketing services provider" or the like make it so. My goal with this book is to help you understand the fundamental business changes that are required to make the transformation possible. These include developing a business plan and a marketing plan, based on the realities of your business—where you are now, what your customers need and the financial realities you are facing—as well as where you plan to go with the transformation. Once the plans are in place, you must not only execute against them but measure your progress against specific metrics along the transformation path. And all the while you must remain vigilant, aware of industry trends, and be flexible enough to make changes along the way as necessary. These steps will give you a greater chance of success.

One thing is clear: Change is the word of the day. There is a great deal of change involved in undergoing this transformation. You must be prepared to embrace that change and lead your team as a change agent. Deciding to make the change is the first step. That is followed by actually making the change—applying the discipline for change, executing the change and keeping the train on the track—all critical elements of success that need to be incorporated into your leadership and management style and process. You should take special notice of the Mail and More story included in this book. This is a company that has embraced change from the outset and has probably undergone more changes than any other single company I have dealt with. Sure, they made some mistake along the way. But in the end, their rapid evolution of the business has paid big dividends.

Change is not easy. But as you will see in the balance of this book, there are proven methodologies that can make it "easier," and give you a greater chance of success in offering, selling and supporting marketing services of various types. There will be failures, and there will be bumps in the road. That *can* be guaranteed. But with proper planning, execution, measurement and refinement along the way, risks can be minimized.

Rome Wasn't Built in a Day

I remember a billboard in Boston during the construction of its famed—or infamous—Big Dig that said, "Rome wasn't built in a day; if it was, we would have hired their contractor." The Big Dig was a massive project that consumed too many years and way too much money. This transformation isn't nearly as gigantic a task, but it can still be a challenge.

I have watched enough companies over the last decade take this transformational path—both successes and failures—that I can see the common threads among successful companies as well as the pitfalls to be avoided. I have also learned by watching these transformations unfold that there are many paths to success, and companies have options in terms of the path they choose. This is certainly not a one-size-fits-all proposition. Building the necessary business and marketing plans is the first step in defining your particular path. Being mindful of avoiding some of the pitfalls described in this book—

learning from the experiences of others—is critical. And doing all of this with both patience and perseverance is absolutely necessary. Using the tools and templates provided in this book will guide you and will provide you with the ability to measure your success as you begin to offer new products and services, changing the way you approach, acquire, manage and retain your customers.

Playing a larger role in the marketing value chain by offering a broader range of marketing services is much different than offering transaction-based business offerings like print, fulfillment and mail. We are not talking "what mailing projects do you have for me today," but rather, we are talking about building long-term relationships with customers who are working with you on a programmatic—rather than transactional—basis. We are talking about getting inside of the customer's head and the customer's business to understand what keeps them awake at night, what business problems they are facing, what needs are unmet, and how you can support them in addressing these issues.

Take your time digesting the contents of this book and defining how it can relate to your business. But once that is done, don't waste any time getting started, either. The window of opportunity is still open, but it *is* closing.

Now let's take a deeper look at some of the drivers that are pushing the mailing & fulfillment industries in a different direction. Then we will delve into what being a marketing services provider means and why you should care.

Does This Sound Familiar?

- Your former competitor closes its doors. A few years ago, you would have been ecstatic, scooping up new clients in droves. But instead, a feeling of unease comes over your company. If this was your primary competition, then what's in store for you?

- The tight economy and the easy access to alternative media that is perceived as less expensive and more effective has clients scaling back on their print needs. This is driving more printers to add mailing and fulfillment services to their offerings. So you start brainstorming how your company can provide additional services to stay in business in the face of new competition from companies who were formerly your business partners.

both marginalized and newly empowered, Internet-connected consumers and business audiences. Determining the right mix of agency, in-house and on-the-ground resources will be an ongoing dilemma as marketers balance creative excellence and campaign ambition with real-world logistics and cultural translation."

This state of disarray and instability between marketers and their traditional agencies opens the door for different types of marketing services provided by new partners in the marketplace and is one reason for the push for mailing & fulfillment operations to transform their businesses and expand their capabilities beyond traditional offerings to address these new opportunities.

Consider this story cited by Bob Garfield in *The Chaos Scenario.* Six Flags wanted to do a promotion for its 45th anniversary to give away 45,000 tickets for opening day to drive traffic. The agency had a brief to do anything it took — ads, web microsites, whatever. The Creative Director posted the offer on Craigslist, and five hours later all of the tickets were spoken for. "No photo shoot. No after-shoot drinks … now the trick is, how do you get paid?"

In his book, The New Rules of Viral Marketing, David Meerman Scott tells the story of the person in charge of promoting the new Harry Potter ride at Universal Orlando. Rather than spending millions of dollars promoting the ride through traditional channels, they used the power of social media. What did they do? They reached out to seven influential bloggers and hosted a webcast. The result? They reached 350 million people.

So while CMO Council research shows that marketers are generally not planning to change agencies, agencies are coming under a whole new type of pressure to deliver services for which many are not prepared. And many of those are struggling to monetize these new services in a way that maintains their profits without gouging their clients. The CMO Council's Marketing Outlook 2010 also reports that most of the actions marketers are taking are tactical, and they are not earmarking funds for back-end process improvement. This has been the case for the last few years, and in fact, building relationships with their CIO/CTO counterparts is not a high priority for most CMOs— only 9% felt compelled to work more closely with these colleagues, according to the CMO Council.

All of this sets the stage for marketing services providers (businesses formerly known as printers, mailers and fulfillment services) to add value to the marketing supply chain in new and unique ways.

So What Is a Marketing Services Provider and Why Should I Care?

While Marketing Services Provider seems to be the most commonly used term to describe this new genre of firm, perhaps marketing communications service provider is a more accurate description, or marketing or business communications service provider. The key is that a marketing services provider is providing a range of services to a marketing department that takes some of the strain off of increasingly limited resources within those marketing departments. These services consolidate programs and campaigns with a single source of responsibility and accountability. We will use the term Marketing Services Provider throughout this book for convenience, but keep in mind the broader definition, and the fact that one marketing services provider's business can and should be very different from another's.

Becoming a marketing services provider doesn't mean abandoning conventional mailing and fulfillment services. I believe these services still have an important role to play in the marketing mix, but marketers don't really spend a lot of time thinking about mail or fulfillment. They are often considered a commodity service to be procured through the purchasing department at the best possible price. And this is a problem for these service businesses.

Consider how decisions are often made about programs or campaigns within a company. First there is a business objective that needs to be satisfied. Perhaps it is conducting an event, launching a new product, driving traffic to a trade show booth or retail outlet, or simply trying to gain more brand recognition within certain target groups. The marketing team will strategize the best way to achieve these objectives. They might bring in their agency or other partners to help with this process. You can bet that most of the conversation will center around digital communications and digital strategies. Then someone might say, "Hmmm…. Perhaps if we included a postcard to drive people to our trade show booth, our retail store, our web site, or even a personalized web microsite, we can get more traction." Hooray! Direct mail just got included, that's the good news. But the bad news is that someone picks up the phone, calls procurement and asks them to get the best possible price on 50,000 postcards, list aggregation and mailing services. Right back to the commodity zone!

When the marketing department turns to partners to help them with these types of strategies, they hardly ever call their fulfillment provider or mail house. Why would they? Do you go to McDonald's looking for Chinese food? So these key services are rarely represented in these discussions.

But they would—and do—turn to a marketing services provider who has established trust and confidence that they know what they are talking about in terms of getting the best ROMI[10] from a campaign or project. They would—and do—if the marketing services provider can demonstrate a way for them to design and test campaigns, monitor results, refine messaging, identify target audiences—you get the picture. Then they don't have to worry about investing in integration of those pesky back-end services with their legacy marketing and enterprise systems, because the marketing services provider takes care of that for them.

But perhaps the best way to describe a marketing services provider is to provide examples of real companies who have made—or are making—the transition. These brief vignettes describe successful companies that will be referenced in various ways throughout the book. The important element to consider when reading these is that they are all very different in their approach to the business, including their business and marketing plans (much more on that later). There is no set template. The category is still being invented. But these firms provide a good perspective on what being a marketing services provider means. In these vignettes, I include some of the individual company history to help the reader better understand where the company came from, its roots and heritage, as well as where it is going as a marketing services provider. Also keep in mind that these companies represent a growing universe of "businesses formerly known as mailers and/or fulfillment services" and are not the only examples out there. We have chosen them for their differentiated strategies and, of course, their willingness to speak frankly on the record.

---

[10] Return on Marketing Investment

Curley Direct Challenges Customers to Think Differently

Family owned and operated since 1990, Curley Direct was originally Curley Direct Mail. Its rebranding was designed to reflect a range of services beyond direct mail in keeping with today's market demands. The company's services include direct marketing communication plans, HP Indigo digital printing, creative, print design, social media marketing, web design, dynamic personalization, cross media, data services and direct mail.

Headquartered in beautiful Cape Cod, Massachusetts, Curley Direct supports clients locally, regionally and nationally with a staff of 15.

"When John [Curley] started the business," says Donna Vieira, Director of Marketing and Communications, "he was in the large print publishing business and had to send out catalogs to aid in the book sales. By day he was selling books, and by night he was running an inkjet machine to address catalogs. He saw the need for consolidated direct mail services on Cape Cod, and thus Curley Direct Mail was born."

In 2006, the company added two Konica Minolta color printers, and in 2008, an HP Indigo. "At that point," explains Vieira, "we knew it was time to show that we were more than just direct mail. We rebranded by dropping mail from our name and are now known as Curley Direct."

With that transition, Curley Direct considers itself to be a marketing services provider. "We don't say we are printers or mailers," Vieira explains. "Our focus is on solving problems for our customers and not just selling them one service. We provide clients with a complete solution based on our services, which include marketing consultation, graphic design, web design, application building, printing, direct marketing, web-to-print and more."

advantage of," Liggett says, "and we opted to go with interlinkONE's SaaS offering." KCI is primarily using interlinkONE for inside storefronts for corporations. "It has been a valuable asset for us," he explains, "especially in terms of inventory management, storefronts, online ordering capabilities, rules-based ordering, and user management. It also drives fulfillment for us, largely literature that we store and fulfill on behalf of our customers."

Liggett points out that most of the company's color work is short-run, and he has been aggressively working with customers to help them understand the benefit of print on demand, rather than print to inventory.

In one example, KCI supports a charter school district with 4,500 teachers whose responsibility it is to market the school to parents. Liggett explains, "The teachers go online, order their collateral through our storefront, and we produce, and fulfill to the teacher. That is more cost effective than printing static materials to a large inventory for fulfillment. It also gives the teachers the ability to customize pieces within established limitations."

Having a marketing automation solution, even though the majority of the revenue is still not going through the system, has enabled Kent Communications to become more engaged in the marketing supply chain. "In the e-marketing area," Liggett says, "we have mini-sites the clients use for gathering a database and then moving it out to another mini site for registration. Or we could have an email promotion where people respond and the appropriate sales professional is automatically notified. There are lots of opportunities a system like this opens for us."

KCI is also working with QR Codes, and in fact, its fleet of vans bears a QR Code. "We are working with clients to develop best practices," Liggett remarks. "Some can be slow to understand their value, but increasingly they are taking advantage of the capability. Our objective is to give respondents a number of ways to respond, whether it be by phone, mail back, through the web, or scanning a QR Code. But the QR Code has to be used correctly—it needs to be backed by a mobile-friendly web site to be effective."

In another QR code example, ArtPrize, a cultural even that takes place in Grand Rapids in the fall, positions a QR code next to each piece of artwork as part of a walking tour of Grand Rapids so visitors can get more information about the artist and what the piece was intended to represent.

In speaking about the challenges he faced in transforming the company, Liggett says, "There has to be a cultural change within the company. That involves having the right leadership and the right people to be able to manage the process." He admits that sales has been the most challenging area, saying, "Some get it and some don't. Our goal is to educate our sales team how to at least recognize the opportunities and understand where these solutions fit. And then we use a team approach with myself and one of our technical people, including the sales person. With this method, we can gradually increase the knowledge level and skill base of our sales force."

In hiring new sales professionals, KCI seeks candidates with a marketing background through LinkedIn, and through networking at local marketing associations. "We use a systematic assessment of our applicants," he explains, "working with a division of Manpower. If after an initial interview we determine the candidate has potential, we work with Manpower's workplace psychologist and use online assessment tools before making a final decision. It is a fairly expensive process, but so is making the wrong hiring decision."

Another challenge is the price erosion in the mail market caused by printers who take on simple mailing projects at a reduced price in order to get the printing business. "We still get the clients coming to us for their data work," Liggett says, "because the printers don't have the capability. But it is difficult to compete with the prices these printer/mailers are charging."

Liggett sees these firms having less penetration in color variable data and more complex variable applications. "Some are getting around this by partnering with mailing houses that don't print. But I believe that is a dying breed that won't be around in another five years or so."

Looking ahead, Liggett says, "There are many unanswered questions about where we need to be in five to ten years. We spend time talking to our customers about where their businesses are going and what they think their needs will be. But it remains to be seen how all of that will shape up."

Mail & More Makes a Direct Impact with Innovation Services

Kim Harrison, Vice President of Mail & More, was on a family vacation in San Diego in 1983, celebrating her graduation from college, when she, her brother Dan, Mom, and Dad visited one of the first Mail Boxes, Etc. stores. This visit stimulated thoughts about starting a new business. They liked the mailing business concept, but felt that the MBE model had no big ticket items to sell. After investigating a Kinko's location that featured large scale copying options, they began to consider the value of combining large scale copying for businesses and consumers with mailing/shipping services.

Back home in Columbia, Missouri, after much research and planning done by Kim's mother, Joy Block, and business counseling from Kim's father, Carl, the family decided to start a business service center called Mail & More. It would offer both mailing and shipping (USPS, UPS and Fed Ex) services, mail box rentals, box sales and packaging and consumer/commercial copying. The first location was a storefront in downtown Columbia. Soon after its opening, Carl's business, Marketeam Associates, a consumer research company located in St. Louis, needed help with mailing services—big time. It had recently acquired Doane Marketing Research that provided much needed agricultural research reports to agricultural services companies. These reports depended on the information collected from Doane's farmer panel in regard to the products purchased for their crop and animal production, like seed, chemicals, equipment and feed. Surveys were mailed periodically to large numbers of farmers throughout the United States and returned by them with the requested information. "Hand mailing work was impossible with these large surveys," Kim explains, "so initially, most of the survey printing and mailing was outsourced." This service void soon stimulated changes in the business plan.

The first change included adding large scale mailing services. A reasonable location was the half of a steel pole barn on the Block farm not occupied by horses and farm equipment. It had a concrete floor and housed some of the operations of Marketeam/Doane. What used to be the garage became home to a Cheshire labeling unit and a six-station inserter. Like the house that 'Jack built,' this building has continued to be remodeled and expanded to accommodate the growing direct mail/document processing/e-commerce/fulfillment offerings of the company. Kim heads this division.

Other changes had to be made. The family determined that the retail business, with its crazy hours, service demands and copycat competition, was too arduous. The growing demand for copy services and commercial mailing services drove them to acquire a local printing company (Brake Printing) and migrate toward an expanded B2B service. These services focus on document design, full color sheet and digital printing and many bindery options. Dan heads this division. "This was way before our trade associations began telling printers to add mailing services and vice versa," Kim says. "We were early in picking up this idea without fully realizing the benefits—that when print and mail are combined, you can control the product you mail, add value to the printed product with your knowledge base of postal regulations, and sell packaged services instead of relying on line item pricing."

The next phase for Mail & More was triggered when a customer needed help inserting and mailing medical statements. "We began to do that," comments Kim, "and all of a sudden we were in the statement processing business. We printed, copied, sent out direct mail and did statement processing. This client also did programming for a Fortune 500 company that had overflow work for kitting and fulfillment--another area we knew nothing about, but we were game."

According to Kim, smaller kit runs used for lead generation were getting lost amidst longer kit runs. "Their operation was designed for longer runs. We stepped in, and now we were in the fulfillment business managing 300 SKUs!" she says.

By the early 1990's, Mail & More realized that using Excel and Access for data management was not efficient and a better way to manage the business operations was needed. Kim says, "We tried a very expensive fulfillment software solution and learned the hard way that if you don't have good systems in place at your facility, the software cannot make them better. You have to have a good operating system in place before you ask the software to fit into your system."

"Housing the software and working the data prompted other IT needs: purchasing servers, hiring a manager, and not really understanding all that was needed to take the business to the next level," Kim reports, "could have put us under. We were lucky at that time because our revenue was greater than the mistakes and our employees worked hard to fill the voids. It was also a good time for mailing as direct mail was being heavily used, and we were working with thousands and thousands of pieces of mail. But we needed to turn our attention to our internal processes and work to get these in order."

The business continued to grow, and as a woman-owned business (Joy Block is majority owner and president), Mail & More was able to secure a contract with the State of Missouri to mail family support statements and support checks. Another inserter was added, and the company found a unique roll-up unit that converted the older inserter into an intelligent inserter that could handle the multi-page statements, barcode reading and more. Mail & More was the only company with intelligent inserting in the mid-Missouri area at the time. "All of a sudden," Kim remembers, "we had too much volume for the two inserters and had to invest $250 thousand in a new one. The next thing we knew, we were truly in statement processing, even adding a bank to our client base."

Meanwhile, as the company had found manual mailing to be too stressful and costly, they were now beginning to see that manual fulfillment processes were cumbersome as well. "In the second half of the 1990s," continues Kim, "we installed interlinkONE to serve our fulfillment needs. In hindsight, we were becoming a leading edge company almost by accident—one of the first to combine mail and print, the first in the area with intelligent inserting, and the first to take advantage of cloud-based services (before anyone was even using the term!) with interlinkONE. Suddenly, we were able to present materials to our customers' remote sales people and agents, allow them to see a thumbnail of the piece, and choose to either download a PDF or have us print their order on demand. interlinkONE allowed us to do that and they were already looking into things we didn't even know we needed yet—landing pages, personalized URLs, QR Codes, and now mobile web pages. They were always a step ahead because it was their plan to do so, but we were able to capitalize on these offerings and land new accounts."

While others in the mail market were struggling to make the shift to a marketing services provider model, Mail & More was, in effect, already there. "But," Kim says, "instead of using the term marketing services, we preferred the term 'visual communications' because everything we do, whether electronic or printed, is visual. Now, we are in the process of rebranding ourselves as Direct Impact, a visual communications company that offers Internet-based and print visual solutions, and one of our strengths in that niche is our distribution capabilities."

Now the company is adding another service; it just signed on its first project that needs call center services. Through interlinkONE, the North Carolina-based call center Mail & More (now Direct Impact) has partnered with, can tap right into order processing to handle customer service inquiries. "This was an exciting experience for us," Kim admits. "We had been giving customers access to their materials, but this was the first time we had given access to a third party."

When asked what the biggest challenge is for the business today, Kim replies, "Educating customers on how to utilize the technology we offer and getting them to change 'business as usual' to try new things. Being from the 'Show Me' state, we tell people and then show them the possibilities. For example, we use QR Codes on our own mailings. We do volunteer work for associations to increase visibility and promote education."

The story of Mail & More is a story of a family business that has been open to new opportunities and responded with market-leading innovation, a company that has been ahead of its time, and delivering unique services that have served its customers well. Its original business plan—being a business service center—allowed for growth and growth includes change. This has to happen if a business is to continue.

As the rebranding to Direct Impact takes effect, its revised business plan will hopefully spur even more rapid growth. A company like Direct Impact, with the 'right' vision and the courage to listen and react to its customers' needs by utilizing the 'right' support services should be able to move forward into the future successfully.

Today's Graphics: Endless Possibilities

Based in Philadelphia, Today's Graphics (TGI) was founded in 1978 as an advertising typographer, a high end type house serving ad agencies and marketing departments of Fortune 500 companies. Founder and CEO Jack Glacken says, "They would give us typesetting, and we would have it done the next morning. We also set ads that were going into brochures, type for brochure mechanicals, labeling for pharmaceuticals, and more. We even used to typeset the headlines for TV Guide."

That's a market segment that is long gone, of course, and TGI has been able to successfully evolve its business through a number of market transitions. Glacken says, "We were the first company in this area to offer color separated films, scanning, and retouching, all on the PostScript side. By the early 1990's, we knew we needed to get into printing, so we merged with a small 2-color print shop and got into digital printing together."

TGI started with a Heidelberg GTO-DI and added 2 Heidelberg 74DI's, which they still have. "We were early into Indigo," Glacken adds, "and we have owned every generation of Indigo they have had."

In those days, a minimum press run was $1,000, and with TGI's digital platform and Scitex RIP, the company was one of the first to offer high quality short run printing at an affordable price. "We underestimated the market demand for high quality short run color," Glacken admits. "Three months into it, we were already where we had projected to be in 28 months!"

TGI later added kitting & fulfillment, serving the pharmaceutical industry with a low-volume operation. In 2010, a large pharmaceutical company client came to them saying, "We are tired of paying for print three times—once when it is produced, once to store, and once to throw out obsolete materials." TGI bid for their print-on-demand/fulfillment business against 13 competitors and won the deal with the support of interlinkONE.

About five years ago, TGI also started looking at mailing. Prior to gaining the large pharma deal, TGI's business was about 85% print, 10% mailing and 5% fulfillment. "This deal will increase both the mailing and fulfillment buckets," Glacken said, "and we have already picked up two more fulfillment accounts.

In the spring of 2011, TGI launched a rebranding effort with an open house, also demonstrating the web-to-print and promotional items capabilities offered by its new marketing automation solution. "We picked up two web-to-print contracts as a result of that event, held on St. Paddy's day," adds Glacken.

TGI was also in touch with a large financial firm in Greensboro, SC who had a third party doing fulfillment in Philadelphia and another party doing the printing. "We were asked to take over the whole thing," Glacken says, "but do it on site in Greensboro. We bought $1 million worth of equipment for that location, and we work with them on a daily basis. We could not have done this without our marketing automation solution." One aspect of that solution that has wowed

TGI's customers is the reporting capability. "They could not get these types of detailed reports from previous fulfillment companies," Glacken says.

Today, the company has 62 employees. "Our revenues were at about $12 million before the recession and dropped to just over $8 million during the slowdown," Glacken explains. "But by 2012, we will be back at the $12 million level."

TGI entered the mailing & fulfillment business from the print side.   Glacken explains that since the company had been doing variable data for a long time, the data issues associated with mailing that can be a stumbling block for many printers did not apply. "But we still have to rely on a mail house for big jobs," he says. "We are not done with mail houses by any means."

Glacken also points out another challenge for 40" shops wanting to get into digital and mailing: Short run is not the forte and their sales people generally don't like selling small jobs. "My recommendation to a 40" printer that wants to get into this business is to partner. Just like I am not doing all of our mailing, and we depend on our mail house for their expertise, a 40" commercial printer should find a trusted partner that can get the learning curve going. If you have 100 jobs per month, in short run it will be 300 or more. You have to have the systems in place to manage a larger number of small jobs. You can't afford a manual process. Take small steps and have a good business and marketing plan; buy one machine and add a sales person that can sell to it. But my advice would be to partner first."

Vision Integrated Graphics

Vision Integrated Graphics is a full-service marketing solutions provider with two locations in the Chicago area. The company has proactively addressed the many changes that have come its way over the past 50 years, including merging the original company, Award/Vision, with Alpha Beta Press in 2005. Today, Vision has 200 employees and revenues of $32 million.

Steve Smits, President, who was with Alpha Beta Press at the time of the merger, says, "When we made the decision to get into digital printing, we knew we also had to get into mailing and fulfillment. They go hand and hand. It is easier to expand across product lines than to acquire new customers. That's why the merger with Vision made sense for us."

Be prepared to Walk it and not just Talk it.

The Great Name Debate

Each of the companies profiled are in some stage of their transformation to what we are calling, for purposes of this book, marketing services providers. From an individual company perspective, some have changed their names and others have not. It raises the question of what these businesses should be called and how they should position themselves.

Do you take the word "mail" out of your name? There is a camp that believes that you have to in order to get access to the C-Suite. As one executive said, "If I go in as a mail house, I get sent down the hall to Procurement. With 'marketing services' in my company name, I have better access and more credibility." Others still depend heavily on mail but have been able to overcome the desire of the C-Suite to shuttle them down the hall.

How do you manage the development of new business while still protecting the legacy business and allowing it to fund new development and innovation? How quickly should you expect this transformation to occur? How do you balance short transactional sales cycles with the long sales cycles generally associated with the delivery of marketing services and other types of solution selling?

These are all important questions that we will begin to address in Chapter Three, continuing throughout the book.

The bottom line, though, is that a marketing services provider helps clients maximize their marketing budgets, as well as generate a better return on investment. Translation –marketing services providers help make their clients' dollars stretch further and deliver better marketing results in the long run.

Keys to Success

- Business transformation requires patience, perseverance and perspective.

- This is not installing an inserter or adding robotics to the warehouse, projects with a beginning and an ending. Business transformation is the beginning of a journey without an end, but with many rewards along the way.

- Business transformation is not for everyone, and there are no guarantees that simply starting down the path will lead to future success. But with proper planning, execution, measurement and refinement along the way, risks can be minimized.

- Becoming a marketing services provider doesn't mean abandoning mailing & fulfillment. To the contrary, your legacy business is both likely to grow and required to fund new business initiatives.

- Building the necessary business and marketing plans is the first step in defining your particular path.

CHAPTER THREE

MAKING SENSE OF THE MARKETING SERVICES PROVIDER TRANSFORMATION

A Deeper Understanding of Data and Campaign Management

While the previous chapter may have been sobering, it leads you to a necessary reality check. Mailing and fulfillment are commodity-based businesses. What I mean by that is that mailing is mailing, and getting products, kits, printed materials and promotional items efficiently in and out of the warehouse is table stakes for the fulfillment business. There is not a lot of differentiation there. Sure, you can present your individual twist on it. You can target a specific market or type of clientele. But in the end, as standalone services, these are commodity offerings. Pure and simple. Sure, you may have a reputation for accuracy and timeliness, for meeting deadlines and drop dates. But if everyone has the same answer to what makes their business different, how much differentiation can that really be?

Being in a commodity-based business isn't necessarily bad. An efficient lettershop can use a variety of techniques to reduce both mailing costs and time to delivery for customers, while at the same time sharing the savings which adds to the bottom line for both the service provider and the customer. But as printers increasingly take on mailing services, these commodity-level services will be the first that they attack, making it more difficult for a dedicated mailing service to survive. As long as a dedicated mailer keeps these risks in mind, perhaps the model will be successful for some time. However, as our case study participants have indicated, now is the time to begin thinking about diversification to lift the business out of that commodity zone into a differentiated space that will sure not only survival, but a profitable business model far into the future.

The same scenario is playing out in the printing industry. It is worthwhile examining one of these "commodity" players that has differentiated itself primarily through high levels of automation. And, oh, by the way, Vistaprint is in the mailing business, too!

Vistaprint: The Ultimate Commodity Printer

Vistaprint is a good example of making commodity printing profitable. The company reported 22% year-over-year revenue growth in its fiscal year 2011 results (ending June 30, 2011), and 16% year-over-year growth in non-GAAP adjusted net income per diluted share. During the 4th fiscal quarter 2011, Vistaprint had approximately 1.8 million new first-time paying customers (important to specify "paying," since Vistaprint does offer business cards free if you pay the shipping and allow them to print their logo on the reverse.) About 68%

Figure 2. Example Branded Customer Storefront

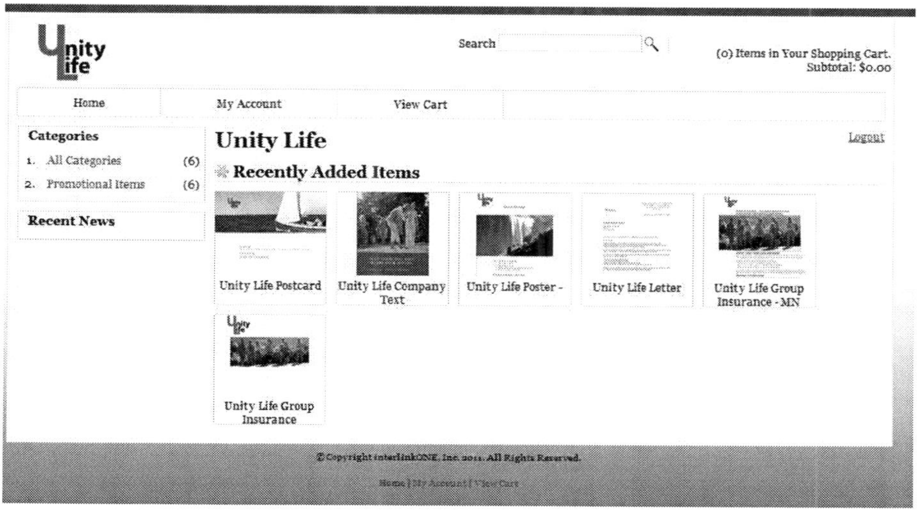

From that point, the service offerings become more complex, but they can be added in easy, manageable phases as you begin to gain more experience with combining printed and non-printed media into integrated, cross-media campaigns, lead generation programs, literature fulfillment and more. Whoa! Wait a minute! Let's read that again. No, I haven't thrown you a curve ball. With the right infrastructure, it is actually that easy to take the next step, and the step after that and the step after that.

Of course, online ordering is a tactic that is an important part of the overall marketing services strategy. You do not want to simply sell one mailing. You will receive far greater benefits by focusing on selling services, including multi-channel marketing campaigns that include multiple mailings, and other channels. If you see someone order one postcard mailing from your store, don't be afraid to ask if there's more behind that order.

Be advised that it is not a good idea to call yourself a marketing services provider before you are ready. Having an online storefront is a step in the right direction, but it is not a transformation. Mailing & fulfillment companies who are not properly prepared, not properly staffed and not properly trained in marketing and who try to sell marketing services may demonstrate a lack of knowledge that could potentially damage the credibility of all.

> ***TIP:** An online store on its own does not identify you as a marketing services provider. It allows folks to do business with you over the web and also would allow their employees to do the same. It only satisfies a portion of the requirement.*

For more information about best practices for providing online ordering solutions, I personally recommend that you check out Jennifer Matt's blog, The Web and Print, at http://TheWebAndPrint.com. You should also consider joining the LinkedIn Group, Beyond Web2Print, which you can find by searching LinkedIn Groups. This group is managed by Jennifer Matt, who is a leading industry expert on the subject.

Online storefronts are rapidly becoming a non-negotiable. You have to have one, but it needs a plan and it should ultimately carry you beyond basic services, into the ability to offer many additional and innovative products and services as well. I personally never fell in love with the term "web to print." I believe we should be thinking about it in terms of web-to-anything. Your web site should allow for any type of request, whether it is for a marketing campaign, a print order, or even an email blast. More on this later. Let's move on to cross-media now.

Cross-Media Made Easy

Before we dive into this section, let's define what cross-media marketing is (with a little help from Wikipedia):

Cross-media marketing is a form of cross promotion in which promotional companies commit to surpassing the traditional advertisements and decide to include extra appeals for their offered products. The material can be communicated by any type of mass media such as e-mails, letters, web pages, or other recruiting sources. This method can be extremely successful for publishers because the marketing increases the ad's profit from a single advertiser.

Furthermore, this tactic generates a good liaison between the advertiser and the publisher, which also boosts the profits.[12]

Some 80% of all printed materials end up in the mail. So adding printing to your business is a logical next step. How much of your mailing work comes from printers? How many of them are looking at supplanting your services by doing the mailing themselves? Just Google "mailing services" on the web to see how many already offer hybrid print/mail. And believe me, fulfillment is not far behind if it is not already there.

As the market consolidates, services are overlapping—there is not the clear distinction there once was. This is driven by printing businesses or start-ups who see the opportunity to expand revenues and margins by adding these value-added services and cutting out the middleman—which is you. And marketers support this type of move from trusted suppliers because it is easier for them to deal with a single point of contact, along with a set of services provided under one roof. Let's take a look at a typical project a marketer might want to produce.

TIP: Go the extra mile...find out more about the life cycle of the stuff you are mailing or shipping. How much gets thrown away? Would they be better served with more targeted materials? How can you help them make the project better, more effective, more profitable—the list goes on—next time?

Marketing Campaign Management and Automation

Driving Traffic to A Retail Store (online or offline!)

In our example scenario, headquarters for a large retail chain is looking for a way to drive increased traffic to both its bricks-and-mortar retail storefronts and its online store. In Chapter Two, we described a scenario where someone in the marketing group decided, almost as an afterthought, to include a postcard mailing in the

---

[12] Source: http://en.wikipedia.org/wiki/Cross-media_marketing

campaign. The difference here is that you—their trusted marketing services provider—are involved at the genesis of the campaign. You are there to advise them and help them get the best return on investment possible, whether it is more Size 10 Nike's tromping into the store to buy something, or Connie Consumer tapping away at her keyboard to buy that something online.

The client has a good mailing list because it has been mailing a catalog. With the rise in postal costs, however, the client is looking for a more affordable way to get the word out. While some email addresses are available, the quality is questionable, so a secondary campaign objective is to update email addresses—which you can't do by sticking an "address change requested" sticker on the email; it either gets to them or it bounces. Well, maybe it gets to them and goes to the spam folder, but that is another issue. So here is the plan you help them assemble:

Figure 3. Sample Cross-Media Marketing Campaign

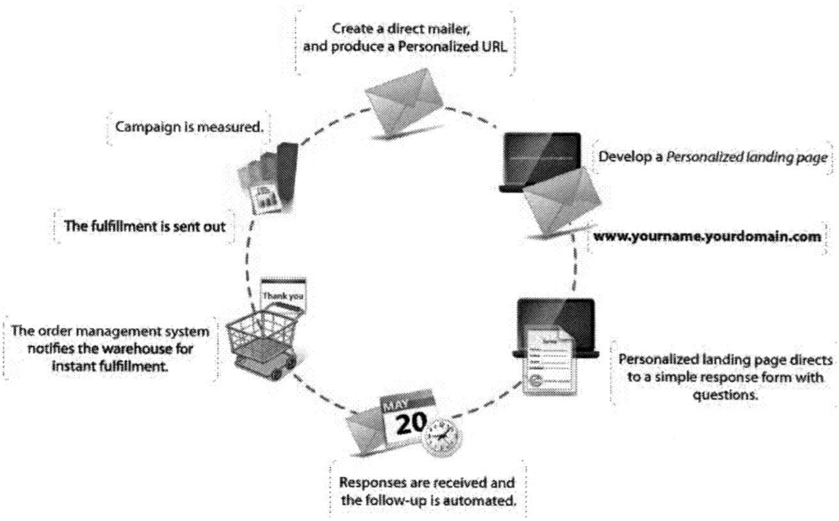

Create a direct mailer, and produce a Personalized URL

Develop a *Personalized landing page*

www.yourname.yourdomain.com

Personalized landing page directs to a simple response form with questions.

Responses are received and the follow-up is automated.

The order management system notifies the warehouse for instant fulfillment.

The fulfillment is sent out

Campaign is measured.

1. Create a personalized postcard with a terrific design and an even more terrific offer. Recipients can respond by going to their personalized URL (www.connieconsumer.retailstore.com) or by snapping an image of a QR code[13] from their phone to

---

[13] A QR Code is a two-dimensional bar code originally created for Toyota's use in parts inventory management in 1994 by Denso-Wave. Codes were designed to have

get there without any typing. Or they can take the postcard to the nearest store. It is even possible to print a map on the postcard showing the nearest store, with driving directions from their home or place of business!

2. Recipients who proceed to their personalized URL by either method may be asked to confirm certain information (including their email address). Information that is contained in the database will be pre-populated on the form. The last thing you want to do is ask for information you have already gotten from them before!

3. Once information is confirmed, they can either take a brief survey to allow you to gather a little more information (brief is key!) and or simply proceed to claim their offer.

4. After two weeks, non-responders are automatically sent a reminder; by email if an address is available, or another postcard for those without an email address in the database. There should be a process in place to catch bounces (rejected emails), remove the offending email address from the database and send a postcard.

5. When an order is placed online, the customer receives an automatic "thank you for your order" email, with a copy to the closest retail outlet. When the customer tromps into the physical store in his size 10 Nikes with the offer in hand, the cashier can scan a code from the postcard to indicate that there has been a response to the offer. The cashier can also try to collect the additional information that would have been captured by the online survey.

6. Or if the customer decides to peruse the retailer's online catalog and purchase online, the order is fulfilled directly by you, with feedback to the retailer about the actions taken.

7. All activity is tracked and available online. The client can view how many people have responded, and by which

---

their contents decoded quickly, thus the origination of QR or Quick Response. Denso-Wave made QR Code technology available as an open platform/open architecture solution rather than maintaining it as proprietary. Today, QR Codes are increasingly targeted at mobile users who can snap an image of the code and have a planned action executed, such as bringing up a mobile-friendly web site (which could be a personalized URL), sending an SMS message, or getting product information or store hours. More on this later.

method. They can see what kind of new information was provided and how many took advantage of the offer or just proceeded to the online catalog and purchased. Also, they can see if any other products were purchased when the offer was redeemed in the store or online (including what they bought and the total amount of their purchase).

8. If the campaign is not delivering as expected, the team (including the marketing services provider) can examine the design, messaging, lists and/or the offer to see if the campaign can be made more compelling.

9. The campaign results (we hope) in incremental profits above what the client was getting from its catalog mailing, including such metrics as an increased response rate, a higher purchase value, and even reactivation of inactive customers.

10. All new data collected is incorporated in the company's Customer Relationship Management (CRM) system and everything is ready for the next campaign. The next campaign might start with an email blast, since now you have updated email address for more potential buyers! For the people that did not opt-in and provide an email address, perhaps you send them a direct mail piece with different creative than the initial campaign.

A couple of points to highlight: You, as the marketing services provider, are an integral part of the campaign from thought to distribution. Secondly, this is a closed loop process. It is not a single mail drop. It is a multiple-touch campaign that sets the stage for the next campaign. This transcends a transactional relationship, turning the customer relationship into a programmatic one that delivers an ongoing annuity stream of new revenues. Both you and the client can monitor progress along the way and tweak the campaigns as necessary. Most importantly, the client is able to meet key objectives— operational efficiency and better support of the sales effort. The client has a clear ROI to take back to the board room. This is a win/win for everyone! Figure 4 reflects what a typical multichannel marketing campaign might look like from a marketer's perspective.

Figure 4. Anatomy of a Campaign from the Marketer's Perspective

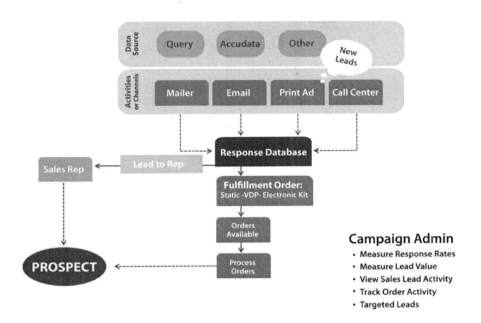

From the marketer's perspective, they may be targeting multiple lists, across multiple channels.

However, to easily measure the effectiveness of the whole effort, a service provider should aim to drive all leads into one database.

This will help to automate the follow-up process, and it will ensure that there is a consistent message being delivered across all channels.

If your business is solely focused on providing mailing or fulfillment services, you may simply be seeing the campaign like this:

Figure 5. Print/Mail-Centric Campaign Participation

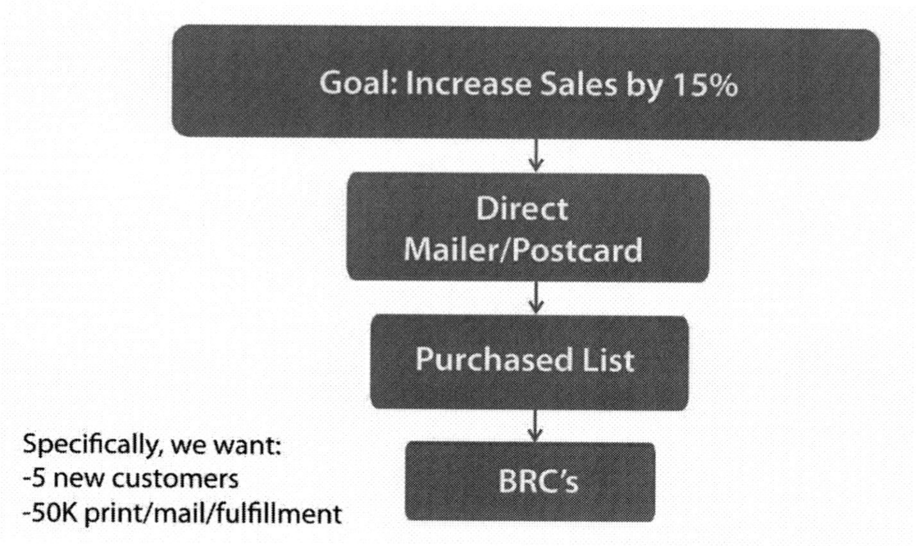

Goal: Increase Sales by 15%
Direct Mailer/Postcard
Purchased List
BRC's
Specifically, we want:
-5 new customers
-50K print/mail/fulfillment

With this view, you only see a campaign with a single leg, or as a one-time event. This is a transactional sale!

From the perspective of a marketing services provider, the execution may be a little different. A good marketing services provider will start by understanding what the client is trying to achieve with the campaign and then help determine the appropriate channel and media mix and strategy to reach that goal. Figure 6 is a flow chart for a typical multichannel campaign from the service provider's perspective.

Figure 6. Multichannel Campaign Flow Chart

Goal: Increase sales by 15%
Direct Mailer
Email Blast
Purchased List
Previous Buyers
Newsletter Subscribers
Previous Buyers
BRC's
Call Center
PURL
Web Registration
PURL

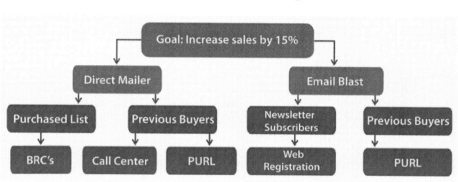

Data is Everything

It is also critical to understand that the marketing database is essential to making an integrated marketing program a win/win. Fortunately, I often speak to folks on this subject. And I guess I do a reasonable job since they still ask me to come speak at their trade shows, events and meetings on just about everything related to marketing. The reason I mention this is when I do speak about marketing data, I always get asked this question: "Where can you get the best marketing database, John?" I always answer: "From the database you build yourself!"

Most people want a magic bullet from a list provider. Yes, you can get good data from a qualified list provider. But it likely will not take into account everything that is relevant to piquing the interest of the target audience. For example, we can get all of the demographic data about someone, including household information, age and more. But can you learn from that demographic data source that they prefer auto racing over boxing?

The idea is to get as close to the data match as you can, and then build your list. Use your marketing skills to build the list, and then personalize it further, beyond simply using their name. That's old hat these days. And continue to enhance that list over time, through multiple campaigns.

As you reach out to the target audience over multiple touches and multiple campaigns, you are establishing a dialog with respondents on behalf of your client. One goal of establishing that dialog with respondents is to gather more information that will make future communications more relevant. By bringing back more information to enhance the marketing database, you and your client will be able to better segment the list, making future communications more relevant. Doing this could help sales as well. How? If we ask qualifying questions over time as we build our list, we help sales by being able to address respondents with more relevant communications that are more likely to encourage a purchase or a positive response to some other call to action.

TIP: You must have the right infrastructure in place in terms of people, process and technology to ensure your role in helping customers build the best databases for their campaigns. You need both marketing and data expertise on board to be a credible resource your customers can rely on.

Our retail example is just one of the many forms a cross-media campaign can take. The possibilities are endless. And new communications media are seemingly emerging every day. In the U.S., for example, which has been slow to incorporate mobile into customer service and promotional messaging strategies, companies are encouraged to begin planning for mobile now[14], and some companies have already made significant progress. In fact, Southwest Airlines, in response to a horrific 2008 hurricane season, started building out a proactive service approach via mobile. By the end of 2009, Southwest had sent more than 5.7 million messages with an error rate of less than 10 percent. While these were customer service messages related to flight cancellations and delays, it is just a matter of time before it becomes common for mobile to be incorporated into integrated marketing campaigns in the U.S. as it is in most other parts of the world. As for Southwest, the company reports that its bill was cut in half by using this automated means of notification rather than outbound calling from its call center.[15]

Multichannel campaigns are not necessarily limited to the types of media we have been speaking about so far. They can also include more traditional media, such as radio, television or newspapers, depending upon the campaign requirements. In the example shown in Figure 7, an athletic club is seeking to grow its membership. Different media are used to reach different target audiences, but the important

---

[14] Customer Service Goes Mobile, 1to1 Magazine, June 2010
[15] Pat Sorce, Director of the Printing Industry Center and Administrative Chair of the School of Print Media at Rochester Institute of Technology (RIT), has written a great book that takes this discussion further. Pick up a copy of her book, "Data-Driven Print – Strategy and Implementation." (Available on Amazon)

element is that each media type has a response mechanism associated with it, so that it is more than simply building awareness—it is a clear call to action.

Figure 7. Building Membership

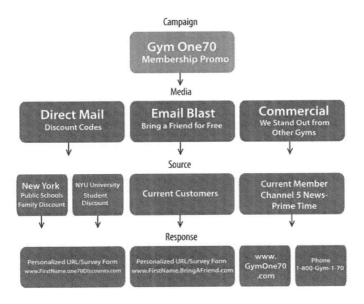

Of course, as the worlds of marketing and communications continue to evolve, charts like the one in Figure 7 will need to be adjusted. You may try putting a QR Code and a personalized URL on the direct mail piece. Also, you may add a leg that starts with SMS/Text Messaging as the medium. The gym may also wish to offer an additional incentive to get recipients to respond; for example, gym-branded tee shirt or water bottle that your organization can fulfill for them. That would add another layer to the diagram in Figure 7. Perhaps the incentive only applies to those who respond to a QR Code or personalized URL, less costly than having someone call the 1-800 number, as further discussed below.

Infrastructure is Key

One of the advantages to Southwest in incorporating mobile into its communications strategy was a shift from direct human interaction to relevant, automated messaging delivered to mobile phones in either text or voice. This type of shift is also available to mailing &

fulfillment providers who have implemented a customer-facing web front end, like an online storefront—perhaps you can use SMS messaging to let customers know a key mailing has been executed or apprise them of some other critical milestone. This shifts the emphasis from human sales interaction (very expensive) to using the Internet for business acquisition. Just like the ubiquity of the Internet does not mean that print is dead or direct mail will go away completely, putting up an online storefront does not eliminate the need for human sales professionals. But it does streamline the ordering process for ongoing customer orders of printed and non-printed items. Customers can even design their own integrated marketing campaigns online if you have the right infrastructure in place. This makes the process more convenient for them and less arduous (and costly) for you.

But online storefronts can also present a danger—inevitably, online storefronts encourage a larger number of smaller orders. If you don't have the right back-end infrastructure in place to handle them profitably, the influx of these many smaller orders can bring you down. What do I mean by that?

If you purchase a standalone storefront offering, a point product that is not integrated well with the rest of your operation, you end up with orders coming in the storefront, being manually retrieved by a human sales professional, customer support professional or other individual, and either being manually placed into a production workflow or manually managed throughout the entire process, depending on your setup. One company I spoke to recently estimated that handling an order in this manner (manually) cost them $40 per order in administrative costs, compared to virtually nothing once they had implemented an integrated order-entry-to-fulfillment system. Now, $40 is not that much if you are talking about a $10 or $20 thousand dollar contract. But it is unsustainable if the average order you are getting is much lower.

It is absolutely vital that you remove as many touches from the order-entry-to-fulfillment process as possible. It is possible to have an order travel all the way from customer ideation to mailing or shipping with virtually no intervention on your part if the system is set up correctly and the order is not extremely complex.

If you are just thinking about implementing an online storefront or your current storefront needs updating, here are some infrastructure considerations to keep in mind as you evaluate new solutions:

- What happens when the order is received? How does it get into production and how much does that cost you from a human resources perspective? Include the cost of errors and rework in this estimate.

- If you are considering a point solution, how easy is it to connect to other applications? That is, are there simple application programming interfaces (APIs) you can use that don't require an IT genius or demand that you continually go back to the supplier for customizations?

- Do customers have the opportunity to do more than upload projects or choose from static catalog selections? While you may not need more than that in the beginning, the solution you choose should be scalable, offering growth opportunity as you and your customers gain more experience with the medium.

- Can you offer electronic downloads of documents, forms and other erstwhile printed materials if a customer doesn't want them printed?

- Will it allow you to do cross-media campaigns? What media are supported, and what is the supplier's plan for the future? This includes the ability to upload and manage lists for postal mail, email and mobile.

- Can you do variable data printing with the storefront solution? This includes the ability to upload lists and database information to be merged with templates to produce graphically rich, personalized electronic or postal communications.

- How about personalized URLs and QR codes? Are those capabilities built in?

- Does the solution have the ability to manage templates? Increasingly, marketers want to control branded materials but give those closest to the customer the ability to adapt materials within corporate guidelines. Templates are the way to get this done.

- Can the solution manage multiple manufacturers? This is important if you want to, for example, add promotional items to your storefront, but you want a partner to do the warehousing and shipping, or if you want to efficiently outsource printing to another business.

- Do you have visibility into all of the transactions processed through the storefront? This includes not only the ability to measure response rates for campaigns, but also the ability to report on who ordered which materials, links back to inventory to make sure supplies stay current, etc.

- Does the solution allow you to easily generate kits? This might include build-on-demand, pre-built, or build-on-the-fly kits. Is the system flexible enough to allow you to generate kits that meet the needs of different verticals?

- Does the storefront support business rules? Can you or the marketer control who is able to order what materials, in which quantities, and whether or not approvals are required for certain transactions?

- Is your storefront easy to configure for other media types as they become a necessity? For example, can you use SMS messaging to acknowledge a customer order or provide shipping information such as tracking numbers?

- Can the solution be easily integrated with warehouse management systems, order processing solutions for picking inventory, and shipping stations?

You may not need all of these capabilities at the outset, but you will be amazed at how quickly you will need all or some of them. You don't want to be out shopping again in a year or two. The key is to make the order-entry-to-invoice process as seamless and error-free as possible, for you and the customer, with as few touches as possible. Without that type of infrastructure in place, don't even think about adding a storefront. Alternatively, there are solutions on the market that can give you all or most of this functionality from a single source. (Of course, I have to mention interlinkONE as an alternative here!)

The Role of Print in a New Media Mix

Clearly, if you have heavy investments in mailing and fulfillment systems—which I assume you do if you are reading this book—you don't want to abandon your heritage in the transition to becoming a marketing services provider. Additionally, if you have not already done so, you should consider adding print to your mix of services in order to provide a more complete solution under one roof. Definitely, you want to build on the knowledge and expertise you already have about your customers and their communications needs in order to deliver a broader portfolio of products and services that will make *you* a trusted partner and *them* a loyal customer.

Protecting that legacy revenue source, while becoming a player in the world of marketing services, can be a delicate balancing act. It is all about positioning—we will talk about that in more detail as we discuss your business and marketing plans in Chapter Four. A key element of those strategies will be your plans for self-promotion as you launch this new aspect of your business. A huge step on the way to credibility is using the tools yourself—walking the talk or eating your own dog food, whichever cliché you prefer. It makes sense to practice on yourself in a safe environment rather than jumping right into customer applications, where a misstep could cost you their business and damage your reputation.

The other advantage of using the tools yourself is ensuring that your employees—and especially your sales force—are comfortable with the process and able to do a good job of explaining the benefits. You can use multichannel campaigns to promote your business, give your sales force access to an online literature library, and even enable your sales force to launch their own campaigns using personalized URLs, QR codes or other tools you have available.

As provider of integrated print/mail services said, "I launched a multi-touch multichannel campaign to promote my business, and a marketing executive I had been trying to reach for some time called me in response, asking, 'Does this stuff really work?' My response: 'You called me, didn't you?'" It works and it will get results—for you and for your customers.

TIP: **We are not talking about doing a self-promotional direct mail piece with personalized URLs once a year. We are talking about an ongoing marketing execution with a pre-planned calendar that is measurable.**

Making Business Communications Interactive

One way to ensure that legacy revenue continues to roll in as you make this transition is to work with your clients on ways they can make their business communications more interactive. As marketers increasingly turn to electronic media, they are seduced by the instantaneous response and tracking and the ability to more rapidly get a dialog going with recipients when using digital media. Your job is to educate them on how to effectively blend direct mail or other printed output into that mix, making their campaigns even more effective than they might be with digital alone. That means making print interactive—giving it the ability to deliver a more effective means of tracking results and a simpler path to getting that dialog going.

According to the DMA,[16] expenditures on direct mail, including catalogs, fell 15.6% from 2008 to 2009. While moderate single-digit growth is expected through 2014[17], this tried and true method of promoting products and services, which had been a reliable business growth opportunity for years for both marketers and mailers, may have finally seen its peak as new media continues to chip away at its presence. But direct mail still has an important role to play, especially when it is combined with multiple other channels of communication and reflects a unified customer experience. And most importantly, when it is interactive.

Most marketers consider print to be a static medium. It is expensive to produce and time-consuming to distribute. It can be difficult to track results of a print-only campaign, and even more difficult to change or refine strategies midstream. This is a misconception. Print can be interactive, cost-effective, trackable and flexible when implemented properly in a multi-touch campaign.

The most common means of making print interactive is by including coupons. If they are appropriately marked with offer codes, bar codes or other means of tracking their source, marketers can measure their effectiveness. But it can take time to tally the results. There are two other tools *available right now* that can include coupons (or not), but also deliver a richer set of results against a wider variety of metrics:

---

[16] *The Power of Direct Marketing: ROI, Sales, Expenditures and Employment in the U.S.*, Direct Marketing Association (www.the-dma.org)
[17] DMA 2011 Statistical Fact Book, Direct Marketing Association (www.the-dma.org)

- Personalized URLs or pURLs were briefly discussed above. These are URLs, or Internet addresses, that are personalized to the recipient (e.g., www.connieconsumer.retailoutlet.com). The recipient is directed to a personalized web microsite directly related to the promotional piece she received, whether by mail or email. The site generally has a similar look and feel to the original communication and can be personalized not only with her name, but also by using demographic, psychographic and other known data about the recipient to make it a relevant experience. The personalized URL establishes a direct link between printed direct mail and the Internet. As soon as a recipient hits her personalized URL, the dialog begins, as does the tracking. It not only provides an opportunity for the recipient to take advantage of a relevant offer, but it also gives the marketer an opportunity to collect more information about the recipient in order that future communications can be even more finely tuned.

- QR Codes: The disadvantage of a personalized URL on a printed piece is that recipients have to key in the address in a web browser. This may involve waiting until they get home or have a break from work, and that may result in the action being sidelined. This can also be true of coupons. This is one reason that QR Codes are becoming more popular in the U.S. (they have already penetrated the market more deeply in Asia and Europe). By placing a QR Code instead of or in addition to a personalized URL on a printed mail piece, you provide the recipient with two options: Either type the personalized URL into a browser, or simply point and click the QR Code with your phone camera to be taken to the exact same destination in a mobile-friendly format. It is easier than typing in the address, it can be done on the run, and it is still unique enough in the U.S. to make people curious to check it out. Once that QR Code is snapped, the tracking of the campaign results begins. Of course, QR Codes can be used for much more than directing people to a personalized URL as part of a marketing campaign. More on that later. (If you are interested in how QR Codes can be created and measured, or are looking for ideas on how they can be used, check out our QReate & Track website at http://QReateAndTrack.com.)

Here is an example of a how a QR Code can be used in a mailer. It contains two ways for people to respond: a personalized URL and a QR Code (which can also be personalized). Download a QR Code reader for your phone and snap this code to see where it takes you! The example QR Codes below the figure also show how you can "dress up" a QR code with color, a logo and more.

Figure 8. Mailer with QR Code and Personalized URL

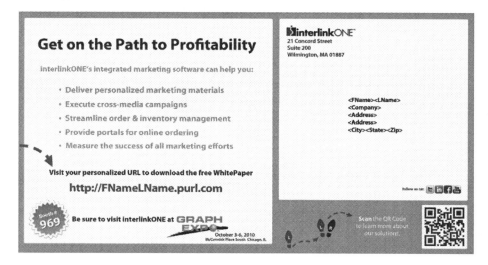

Figure 9. Two Different Types of QR Codes

By first using these techniques in your own promotional efforts, and then by working with customers to integrate them into theirs, you are on your way to becoming a marketing services provider! See how easy it can be?

Mobile Marketing

The DMA reports declines in direct mail, as mentioned above, with modest (1.1%) increases in Internet marketing from 2008 to 2009. Mobile marketing, albeit on a much smaller base, grew at 46.9% during the same period, 50% between 2009 and 2010, and is targeted to grow as much as 25.2% between 2010 and 2014!

One major reason for this growth is the increase of smart phone sales. I believe smart phones have changed the game, and will continue to do so as they become more ubiquitous and feature-rich. Nielsen forecasts that 1 in 2 Americans will have a smart phone by Christmas 2011, up from just 1 in 10 in the summer of 2008.[18]

What's a Smart Phone?

Just to clarify, Wikipedia explains that a smart phone is a mobile phone that offers more advanced computing ability and connectivity than a contemporary basic feature phone. Smart phones and feature phones may be thought of as handheld computers integrated within a mobile telephone, but while most feature phones are able to run some applications, a smart phone allows the user to install and run more

---

[18] *1 in 2 Americans Will Have a Smartphone by Christmas 2011,* by Kevin C. Tofel, gigaom, March 26, 2010.

advanced applications based on a specific platform. Smart phones run complete operating system software providing a platform for application developers. A smart phone can be considered as a Personal Pocket Computer (PPC) with mobile phone functions, because these devices are mainly computers, although much smaller than a desktop computer or tablet. Additionally a PPC (Personal Pocket Computer) is more personal than a desktop computer.

With the growing supply of smart phones, including Apple's fourth generation iPhone (despite its early antenna problems), Google's Android, the ubiquitous Blackberry and more, we are becoming an increasingly mobile society. We expect to have connectivity anywhere and everywhere. And not just for phone calls. Want quick ideas on a new restaurant in your area or in a town you are visiting? Just visit Yelp.com on your iPhone. Looking for the closest Home Depot? Google Maps can help you with that, and you don't need to sit down at your computer. Check it out on your Android. Want to cash in that coupon? Unilever's mobile coupon trial lets consumers redeem coupons by having a supermarket cashier scan their phones—a successful trial will surely push this capability quickly to mainstream. Faster boarding at the airport? Download your boarding pass to your smartphone and eliminate paper boarding passes or the need to check in with an agent before going through security.

As a mailing & fulfillment operation transitioning to the delivery of marketing services, mobile should surely not be overlooked. Marketers are proceeding cautiously with mobile investments, particularly in the U.S., but they are moving nonetheless.

TIP: Warning: Stay current or be left behind!

One aspect of the intersection of mobile computing and marketing is the use of QR Codes, described above. Perhaps QR Codes will be the "killer app" for the addition of mobile to the media mix. And the good news about QR Codes? They generally are printed before they are snapped! This technology ties print into other communications channels and is an ideal way to get started with multichannel campaigns. Also, since QR Codes are just beginning to catch on in the U.S., you can be a hero by introducing the concept to your customers—ideally through a self-promotional campaign that introduces your new capabilities and reminds folks of all of the other things you already do so well for them. A key success factor with prospects and customers is your ability to demonstrate your vision about new techniques that can help your customers perform better and measure their marketing efforts more effectively. QR Codes may be the easiest way to dip your toe into the waters.

There is no question that mobile marketing is well on its way to becoming mainstream. Most folks I know practically sleep with their phones! Or at least they have them at the ready an arm's length away. I believe that every transitioning printer needs to understand this part of the marketing mix and how it fits into not only their business but the lives of their customers. If we are already talking about QR Codes or text messaging or even emails, we are talking mobile. I asked a service provider the following question:, "Do you think people search for your company on their mobile devices yet?" One said, "Yes, I think people search for information they are looking for on their mobile devices, and I hope I come up." I said, "Great answer. Now, is your company website mobile ready? Is your sales team? Are your marketing efforts?" Just like that he froze and said, "I never even thought about it."

Here is a link to a great resource to build your mobile site and other mobile ideas: http://ilnk.me/iMobile

By the way, do you own a smart phone? If not, you should!

The Importance of Listening

One of the most difficult transitions for most traditional mailing & fulfillment firms to make as they migrate to selling marketing services is transitioning to a new sales process. We will talk about that in depth in Chapter Eight, but it bears mentioning here as well. One of the pitfalls to avoid in transforming your business is lack of awareness and understanding of the needs of marketing departments. Chapter Two discussed the needs of marketers at a macro level, but of course, every company is different and each marketer will have a different twist on the needs and pain points in his or her daily life.

Companies who have made the transition will tell you that most traditional sales reps have a difficult time moving from the "what project do you have for me today" model to the solution selling model required as a marketing services provider. In Chapter Two, Vision Integrated Graphics Smits reported that only about 20% of the sales force can sell solutions. He uses his traditional sales force to uncover the opportunity but then use a solutions sales specialist and/or technical resource to follow up, and this model has proven to work for other companies as well.

The first sales call when addressing an opportunity in the marketing department should always be a listening call, not a selling call. This is the best way to learn about the customer. This first listening call should be followed by a second visit that offers a solutions approach to solving the issues you learned about in the first call. Remember, if you start talking about solutions (mailing/fulfillment) without first understanding the issues that *need* to be solved, you will be shuttled down the hall to Procurement, and that is not where you want to be.

When you do go back for the second call with a vision of what you can offer this particular client to relieve or eliminate pain points, the vision must be well beyond individual point solutions, like personalized URL's and emails. You must be thinking of integrated, multi-channel marketing campaigns and measuring the results.

TIP: Warning: To do this requires a skill that most sales people still need to develop.

An effective marketing services provider must understand how a prospect or customer typically produces marketing campaigns as well as how to help make them more effective through involvement with the entire marketing campaign. Now you are offering a solution that can develop into a long-term relationship versus a commodity-based transactional sale that you have to re-sell every time. Two very different situations. But it all begins with listening.

marketing services provider. They talked about the need to have certain point solutions, such as personalized URL's, web-to-print and workflow. I asked them where they were going after they left our stand and they told me they planned to see the usual vendors, each having this or that piece of the puzzle. They indicated that their business was not doing well, that they didn't think they had the right sales professionals in place, and that they needed both a new sales team and software solutions in order to make their transition to a marketing services provider.

Then I asked them where their marketing person was, and they informed me that they didn't' have one, and they didn't do any marketing! While I remember this conversation specifically, it is not an unusual occurrence during a trade show—or general sales—conversation, I am sorry to say. What I told them, and what I have told others, is, "Stop right there. You don't need a new sales force or new software solutions to begin your transformation. You need a marketing professional on staff, period. Then you will have the resource to support sales and help you acquire the right tools to execute upon your new business strategy. You can't buy my software today, and I recommend that you don't purchase anything else until you have that marketing person in place to help and guide you."

> **TIP:** *It is critical to have the right resources in place in order to make your business transformation successful.*

It may seem a little strange for me to be at a trade show pitching my software, yet tell a prospect, in essence, to go back and do their homework before they can buy anything from me. But had they purchased my solution—or anyone else's for that matter—their chance of success with it was slim. That is a sale not worth making. I asked them to imagine me, a software vendor and a technology guy for over 20 years, deciding that tomorrow, I would go into the mailing business and I needed to purchase automated inserter. I can tell you right now that I am not qualified to do so, and doing so would be a sure recipe for disaster. Our conversation ended amicably. They agreed with me and went on their way. I am not sure what they ended up doing, but I hope I helped them avoid the biggest pitfall of all—making marketing-oriented decisions without the advice of a marketing professional! The moral of this story? You need the right resources in place to execute on a strategic plan. If the strategic plan is marketing-services oriented, you need a marketing professional, either on board or as a close partner, to begin making that transition. We will discuss this in more detail later in the book.

Keys to Success

- What differentiates you from your competition? Service, Quality, Price? If everyone has the same answer, how much differentiation can that really be?

- Building the necessary business and marketing plans is the first step in defining your particular path to transformation

- Becoming a marketing services provider doesn't mean abandoning your current services. Protecting that legacy revenue source while becoming a player in the world of marketing services is critical, but can be a delicate balancing act.

- Having an inviting and easy-to-use online ordering solution makes your business more accessible to today's buyers of business communications services.

great deal about order management, business rules, who can order what and how many, how an order goes through the shop floor, kitting, pick/pack, shipping, etc. Financial services is a highly regulated industry, and we determined that we should leverage our industry-specific knowledge in that vertical market in our sales and marketing efforts. In addition, being located in the Boston area, we had a heavy population of high tech companies right outside our door. Based on those and other considerations, we determined that we would focus our efforts on two industries: high tech and financial services. We tightened up the business plan to address those verticals; that got us back on track, and we began to gain traction in our chosen markets.

This experience reinforced for me the importance of the business plan, especially the marketing component. It also reinforced the fact that the business plan must be a living, breathing, evolving thing. That is especially true of the marketing portion of the business plan. There is no end to the need to review and update marketing strategies; it is an area that is always evolving and changing, and it needs constant reflection and review to ensure that it stays current with changing market needs.

Another's Personal Experience

My good friend Peter Muir of Bizucate was kind enough to share some of his wisdom and experience on the importance of a business plan and marketing plan. Scan the QR Code below to see an exclusive video of Peter discussing that topic:

Change is Constant

I am not a warm-and-fuzzy or philosophical kind of guy, but I was and am always big on change. I have no problem with a new tool, a new application. For example, I have had an Apple iPad for some time now. As an early adopter of tablet technology, I have had a lot of fun, learned a great deal, and gained some advantages. My perspective is, if we try something new and it doesn't work, we have learned something. Some people don't like change, and that can be an issue in this environment. Others are simply reluctant to take risks, preferring to rely on "tried and true," which just doesn't play in a dynamic market such as we are faced with today.

I continually strive to take steps to ensure that a culture of change exists at my company, interlinkONE. In fact, one of my most famous tactics took place a few years ago. I thought we had some change-resistant folks in our organization. Yes, it happens; and yes, change is difficult for most. The comfort zone is the easy way out. So what did I do about it? We gathered everyone for a company lunch and update meeting on a Friday afternoon. When they picked up their slices of pizza, each employee received a copy of the book *Who Moved My Cheese* by Spencer Johnson, M.D.

Employees were required to read this book by Monday morning. Sure, the homework assignment may have induced a few groans, but that book does a wonderful job of simplifying the need for employees to be ready for change. If you haven't read it, I highly recommend it. It is a fable-oriented book that helps people manage change in their work environment or in their personal life. Fun to read but with lots of meaningful content.

When I started interlinkONE, print, email and the web were a great combination. But now we also have to include social media and mobile in the mix. Who knows what will come next? The important thing is to have a good, solid business plan with a strong marketing component, and to be vigilant and flexible in keeping it up to date. Use the business plan as the guiding light, but don't consider it set in stone. It can be changed. But you do need to start somewhere.

TIP: Revisit your business plan on an annual basis at a minimum. Measure the results you have achieved against the business plan objectives. Did you achieve what you said you would?
CAUTION: Your business plan must have a well-thought-out framework; you don't want to end up in a business-plan-of-the-month ritual!

In our case, we learned from our earliest attempts that you can't be all things to all people. We didn't have a centralized focus. We were selling to anyone who would talk to us. As a result, we spent way too much time educating and not enough time closing sales. The only reason we are still here today is because we had a business plan in the first place, and we looked at it on an annual basis. We measured our results, and when we were not meeting our targets, we stopped and reevaluated who was our best target audience for the solution we had developed. Once those targets were determined, we looked at the growth potential in those industries. That included an evaluation of inhibitors we might face in selling into those industries. That, in turn, resulted in a need to modify our marketing plan to address those inhibitors.

One thing we did learn in our early sales efforts was that when marketers understood what our solution could do for them, they would get very excited. The barrier we hit more often than not was the IT department because we were an externally hosted solution, something IT departments were not that fond of in those days. It was not like we were hosting Microsoft Exchange or Word. This was a mission critical application—business and market intelligence. IT professionals are always cautious, as they should be, and we needed to ensure that we had our ducks in a row to be able to convince them that hosting was the right answer for this particular application.

Business Plan as Funding Vehicle

This was all happening in 1999 and into 2000. At the same time we were revisiting our business plan, we also determined that we wanted to gain outside funding to help us grow faster. That was another objective in revisiting the business plan—making sure it was updated and attractive to potential funding sources.

Sometimes it is better to be lucky than good, although I prefer it when both line up. We had raised $2 million in financing by the time the dot-com bubble burst in about March of 2000. We had no crystal ball that told us what was coming. But had I approached the financial markets with a plan that had them filling the bucket in six months rather than immediately, it never would have happened. (Lucky.) Had we not had great customers—some marquis brands that were direct customers—we probably would not have made it through the turmoil, either, because we had this stigma (being a hosted web software service) that we had to get around for new clients that extended the sales cycle. (Not good, but manageable.) I remember saying to my sales team back then, "Man, it is hard enough to sell one thing, never mind having to educate them and sell them on hosting (outsourcing) the software as well."

For us, the stars aligned, and it had a great deal to do with the quality of our business plan and our relentlessness in measuring ourselves against the objectives laid out in that plan. We also kept an eye on our marketing objectives, and we made sure that everyone in the company was marching to the same drummer as we spoke to and served customers.

Riding a Roller Coaster

A year later, we were riding another roller coaster—after 9/11, everything came to a screeching halt. No sooner did I see a bit of reprieve coming than we were hard at survival again, revisiting our business and marketing plan once more. This time, we determined we could make more headway by building a channel strategy rather than selling direct, a fairly significant change in business model. Because of my background in working with fulfillment houses, we chose service providers as our channel. In our minds, that included fulfillment houses, mailing houses and commercial printers.

What I didn't understand then—but understand quite well now—is that fulfillment operations have a different mindset than a commercial printer or a mailing house. In many cases, fulfillment service providers already have a relationship with the marketing departments of their customer's businesses. Thus, fulfillment houses were early adopters in implementing our solution. They already had infrastructure in place to address regulatory requirements, as one example.

One California-based company that was an early adopter was able to use our solution to fulfill documentation and notifications for a major online stock trading company. Here's how it worked: An email containing important stock information was sent to each person on the list. If an email bounced, the fulfillment company had to be prepared to automatically send a hardcopy in order to comply with regulations, and our solution supported that. Our system sent the email blast...it also provided reporting and tools to manage the bounces. It generated the necessary orders for hardcopy documents, including the pick ticket, packing slip, and shipping label.

Fulfillment companies also saw the value to the customer of these services and knew how to charge for them. They didn't give them away. In addition, long before the marketing services transition began in commercial print, fulfillment houses were already diversifying—buying presses, adding mailing equipment, and more.

As we revisited our business and marketing plan, it was clear that fulfillment houses would be a terrific channel for us. We also looked at the commercial print segment, and like many before us, were attracted by the huge number of establishments—and the assumed market opportunity that represented over the long term. We knew, however, that it might be a longer educational cycle for a large percentage of commercial print establishments, and therefore, our plan was designed to help us seek out the early adopters in that segment who were already providing some level of marketing services and were already talking about, or in the process of, transforming their businesses. These firms were looking for innovative solutions to help with that transformation. By working with them, we were able to get a foothold in the commercial print industry while we continued the education process with the mainstream adopters.

These are the kinds of discussions you must have with your team as you revisit your business plan annually—did we accomplish what we said we would? If not, why, and how can we remedy that? If so, how can we do even better in the coming year? Are there new markets, new channels, we should be going after? It takes vision. It takes hard work. It requires staying current with market trends. And it means having a cohesive team that supports the strategies comprehended in the business plan.

When was the last time you revisited your business plan? Was it within the last year? If so, great! If not, now is the time. Or perhaps you don't have a business plan or a marketing plan in place. This is the ideal time to remedy that. I know, based on the calls I get, that there are many companies in our industry that do not have a business plan, let alone a marketing plan. I had a call from a business owner telling me he wanted to begin using personalized URLs; he wanted to know what he should charge. I thought, "Why would he ask me that?" Clearly, there was no business plan in place. The pro forma financials had never been done. They had not done the hard work to understand the market opportunity for this new service.

As we researched the industry and began to understand that most traditional print and mailing service providers do not have a business plan in place, we wondered why? How and why would you run a business without a business plan? By asking around, the reason became clear. First and foremost many printing and mailing companies have been around for a long time, and many of them have been passed down through family members. The plan in place is the "that's the way we've always done it" plan. The other reason we've found for the lack of business plans is that traditional printing and mailing companies that started 50 to 100 years ago didn't need one. The plan was to sell print. The market was local. And the need for a business strategy wasn't present. Printing and mailing companies didn't even have a large need to market themselves in the past.

It was easy—a printer or lettershop hung out a shingle that read "printer," or "mailing services," purchased a Yellow Pages ad and listing, and it was pretty self-explanatory what they offered to the market. Some did different forms of printing and mailing, but the offerings were easily identifiable and it was easy to let people know you were a printer or mailer and open for business. Times have changed; this model simply does not work anymore, for either type of business.

So in some cases, the reason for a lack of a business plan was because companies may truly have not needed one to survive. As family businesses were passed down from generation to generation, along with inheriting equipment, the next generation also inherited customers, processes, and other resources that helped ensure that the business could stay above water. However, as we have been discussing, as the world of marketing and communications has changed, service providers can no longer ignore the importance of a business plan.

In addition, mailing companies are very good at analyzing whether or not they should purchase an inserter or inkjet solution. A company that wants to enter the variable data printing market, for example, can easily determine which digital press or inkjet add-on to buy, how many people it will take to operate it, what the consumables will cost, how many sales people they need, and whether or not they can make a profit.

Offering marketing services is very different from buying a press, inserter or inkjet solution, however. The analytics are not always as clear-cut. Each service must be a line item in the business plan and in the pro forma financials. But there are also many costs that must be incurred before you can even consider making the first sale:

- You need to buy the solution(s) to support the proposed services.

- You must have marketing resources on staff and/or a firm partnership with a marketing services agency.

- You may require the services of a consultant to advise you in constructing packaged services, doing market research or other things.

- How will you handle creative services? Will you design in-house or will that be an outsourced service?

- How will you get the business started? How will you promote it? How will you build recognition and credibility for your new business?

- How will you price services, and how many of each line item can you sell each month? What people do you need to hire to support this growth?

- How are you going to measure results, for you and for your customers?

All of this is required before the first sale is even contemplated. "How much do I sell a personalized URL for" is a question that comes from someone who is still in the transactional selling mode and has not done their homework on the business and marketing plan. It is still selling a point solution. It is still a one-time transaction, not taking into consideration the full business opportunity surrounding the use of personalized URLs within an integrated communications plan, including campaign development, management and tracking. And suppliers who recommend selling personalized URL's at 8, 10 or 12 cents a pop are not doing you any favors, either.

So let's go through the business plan, item by item. Using this as a guide will put you on solid footing as you begin the transformation. If you already have a business plan in place, perhaps now is the time to revisit it, and this guide will help with that as well. It is structured to drive strategic thinking and should not be considered as a form-filling exercise.

The Step-by-Step Breakdown

When you make the decision to undertake the transformation to a Marketing Services Provider, you are not alone. There are companies and resources available to help make the transition as seamless and pain-free

them if you haven't worked with the system yourself? You need to understand the basics of marketing and help your clients create marketing plans if they don't already have them. Don't worry – we have marketing plan templates available in our online resource center that can help you with this challenge.

TIP: *If you do not do this, your employees will be slow to embrace this change, and your customers will be slow to adopt. You will have less chance of rapid success.*

[Your Name Here] Business Plan

The full business plan should be no more than 15 to 20 pages. This forces you to write it carefully, resulting in a thoughtful, concise plan that is extremely easy for any business person to follow, whether or not they are familiar with your business or industry. A detailed template is available online at http://www.NewPathToProfit.com.

TIP: *Avoid the use of industry-specific or company-specific acronyms in your business plan.*

Introduction

This section should introduce your company as it is today, and as you anticipate it will look in the future. Following are a number of topics that can be addressed in the introduction to your business plan.

- Business goals/mission

- Business description
- Date of business formation
- Business philosophies/identity, including culture
- Location
- Directors
- Management team
- Key competitive advantages
- Strategic positioning
- Strategic alliance(s)
- Sales summary
- Vision of the future and primary objectives of business transformation
- Resources required (Capital, Human)

Product and Service Mix

You must clearly identify the products and services you will be selling in this new business. This section of the business plan spells those out in detail; the marketing plan, which we will address later, spells out the execution—your go-to-market plan for selling these products and services.

Typical products and services included in a marketing services provider business plan include design and deployment of multichannel marketing campaigns, creative services, data management and analytics, tracking and reporting, ROI analyses, to name a few. Some companies add items like promotional products, signage and display graphics, audio, video, and building a social media presence or online reputation for the brand. These can be services you offer yourself, or that you outsource to a third party (as in the case of promotional products). In your off-site workshop, you and your team will have brainstormed the products and services that could be included in the mix and boiled it down to the critical few that will form the backbone of your new business initiative.

For each product/service, the business plan should reflect sales estimates. How many can you realistically sell per month, per quarter? To help you develop this piece of the business plan, an Excel spreadsheet is available online at http://www.NewPathToProfit.com. It will form the foundation for the financial plan included later in the business plan. For example, if you will be offering video services, how much will you charge per hour? At what point do volume discounts kick in?

Cross-media programs may encompass a number of line items, including:

- ***Consulting services:*** How much will you charge per hour? How many hours do you anticipate being the norm for an average cross-media project?

- ***Target audience identification:*** This involves working with clients to help them refine the target audience for their campaign based on their go-to-market strategies, data available within the enterprise, data available externally, etc. List development, hygiene, and management could be included here. For an average cross-media program, how many hours do you expect to consume, at what rate? What revenue will you receive from sources such as mark-ups for list purchases?

- ***Creative services:*** Will you be doing the design, or does the client have other resources? If you are responsible for the design but outsourcing the work to a partner, what is the revenue model between you and the third-party designer?

- ***Campaign deployment:*** This includes printed and electronic distribution of the campaign.

- ***Personalized URLs, QR Codes and other variable data elements.*** How much will it cost you to generate personalized URLs, QR Codes or other variable data elements, and how much can these be sold for? When will volume discounts kick in?

- ***Audio/Video services:*** What percentage of the campaigns do you anticipate will include audio/video? Will you be generating these elements yourself or outsourcing them? What is the revenue model?

- ***Tracking and Reporting:*** Depending upon the solution you have in place, the marketer may be able to go online and see the results for herself. There is a value associated with that capability. It could be in the form of a monthly service charge. Perhaps there is a set-up charge associated with building a customized dashboard for each specific client/campaign. Even if the marketer chooses to monitor campaigns herself, you will likely want to generate your own reports for her to reinforce the results you are achieving and your value as a partner.

While you will need to do a pricing exercise for each of these line items, the price to the client should be bundled as a package to eliminate the tendency for clients to pick certain elements, such as print, and try to commoditize them.

Let me provide you with an example that might help crystallize your thinking around how to package these services. Let's say you are working with a client in a campaign whose objective is to sell Steve Madden sunglasses.

- First you need to work with the client to identify who is most likely to purchase these sunglasses—the anticipated target audience. It may be based on factors such as gender, age, and where they live. It might take eight to ten hours of consulting to determine the target audience and where you will acquire the lists to address that audience.

- Perhaps there are another three hours devoted to campaign management.

- Also, you may need to account for another four hours that will be spent on the reporting and analysis for the campaign.

These are consulting services not directly related to the actual production—print and/or electronic—and they have a market value. With respect to the consulting services, you must recognize what steps you need to take to offer valuable answers and insight. You do not have to be the expert in your customer's industry, but you need to take some action so that you understand their business. This will require hours, and there should be a fee associated with those hours, whether you do this by yourself or with others.

You might ask: How will I know this if I have never done it before? Try doing a self-promotional campaign to see what is involved. You can do this on your own or with a partner. It will not only help your existing business, but it will give you good insight into what is actually involved in developing and deploying a cross-media campaign. In addition, if you have your marketing professional on board, they will have experience in pricing the proposal.

When it comes to laying the groundwork for the reporting and analysis that you will provide to your customer, there is one thing that I want you to keep in mind: Promise that you will *measure what you did*, but avoid guarantees of specific success.

TIP: *Make sure you have someone on staff that can support you and your clients in the reporting and analysis process.*

You can do these computations on a cost-plus basis—that is, how much it costs you to deliver the services, plus the margin you expect to achieve—but that is not the best option. You should be thinking about value pricing. For example, in the financial services industry, the customer may be trying to increase the number of enrollments. If you know the value to the client per enrollment and the impact each has on the client's revenues, you can calculate the value if you are able to increase enrollments by 1%, 2% or 5% (keep your estimates conservative, at least in the beginning, to keep customer expectations in line). Remember this when proposing these solutions — under-promise and over-deliver. Those calculations give you a basis for value pricing.

Additionally, as you are working through the definition of these programs, keep in mind that people don't typically buy based on one touch. You can do a radio commercial for the sunglasses that directs people to go to a specific URL, and that might generate a few leads. But for best results, it is a multi-touch, nurturing approach that delivers results. Figure 11 shows a typical sales and marketing funnel starting with the initial large pool of targeted potential buyers, qualified leads based on responses, and developing those leads into a sale through a multi-touch process.

Figure 11. The Sales/Marketing Funnel

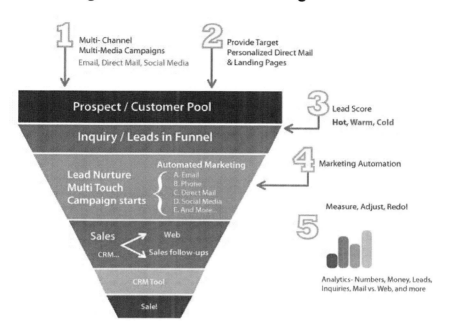

In our sunglasses example, we might start with announcing the offer on the radio. At the same time, we could send an email with a personalized URL to a targeted group of college students. Non-responders might get a postcard. Responders can be taken to the next level in the sales process, perhaps with a discount coupon they can download to their mobile phones if they refer a friend.

In the value pricing model, what is the value to the client for incremental sales of the sunglasses? Even better, what is the lifetime value of a consumer who buys one pair of Steve Madden sunglasses? How many more are they likely to buy over their lifetime? If your audience is 1,000 students, how many pairs of sunglasses will be sold? All of these factors should be considered in a value pricing model. If you simply mark up the cost of your services using a standard margin, you are selling yourself short and reverting to a transactional, rather than a solutions-oriented, model.

This is different than the budgeted hourly rate for a piece of equipment on the production floor. This is not like preparing a direct mail project, where you have to call out every line item because you have always been required to do so. This is a whole new game. Just be careful to structure the proposal to avoid scope creep. For example, if video is included, three hours might be bundled in, with a footnote that if it exceeds three hours, the cost will be $XX per additional hour.

Still dubious that this can work? Consider an agency: They sell the value by promising an increase in awareness of this much, an increase in leads generated of that much, and they sell the program for $20 thousand with a strict limit on the number of edits allowed. That doesn't even include the cost of printing. It's just the creative. Agencies have been doing business this way for decades.

But while you do want to make a good profit, it does have to be reasonable and you have to be able to justify it to the client based on the value they will get in the end. If you are going to sell 453 pairs of those sunglasses to your list of 1,000 students plus referrals to their friends, what is the incremental value to your client? If you know that, you will know what a reasonable value-based price is for the campaign.

One thing I want to caution transitioning marketing services providers is to never promise an increase in response rates through the use of multi-channel marketing. The goal is to be able to measure multi-channel marketing results, good or bad. It is certainly good as a sales tool if you can cite studies that reflect the lift that multi-channel can achieve, but saying it will happen and guaranteeing an increase is a danger. Knowing how a campaign did, knowing which methods worked better, and having actionable intelligence is the key, not guaranteeing results that the campaign may not be able to deliver, often for reasons beyond your control.

However, you can promise that you will build intelligence and measurement into each and every campaign. This is one of the things lacking in many marketing departments. When you can provide this information for them, you will be able to perform the next campaign based on facts, growing a solid experiential base over time.

Next in this section of the business plan is a *market analysis*. What vertical markets or specific industries will you pursue with your marketing services? What types of companies need these services based on management team, business size or other factors? Smaller companies are typically more under-resourced and underfunded in the marketing arena than larger companies, so perhaps they are your first target. What geographic reach are you planning for and how many of these companies are there within that geography? That becomes your addressable market. And then realistically, what percentage of the addressable market do you think you can capture?

Over the years we have seen industries where our customers have had more success than others. Perhaps you will, too. Some of those industries are:

- Education (K-12 and Universities)
- Real Estate
- Pharmaceutical
- Manufacturing

You also will want to do an analysis of your current customer base. By analyzing customers you know, you can build profiles for like customers that you can add to your prospect base.

A section on *marketing goals and strategies* is also recommended. How will you market your new business, and how will you measure your success? Brainstorm with your team what you want to get out of this effort. Interestingly, this effort will help you in your sales strategies, because this is exactly the same challenge your customers are facing. Marketing goals might include:

- Building awareness of your new business and capabilities
- Increasing traffic to your web site
- Adding [pick a number] new customers
- Getting a certain number of marketing services customers to ante up for repeat business

What are the strategies you can employ to achieve those goals? This can include direct marketing, advertising, trade shows, online marketing—these are all strategies. At the business plan level, you will spell out goals and strategies; at the marketing plan level, you will spell out the execution details, the specific tactics you will employ.

The business plan should also include a *competitive analysis*. In the age of the Internet, this is easier than it would have been in the past. But you must also look beyond your traditional competition. Start by looking at other mailing & fulfillment companies in your geographic area; are any of them transitioning to marketing services providers? For most companies making the move, these local competitors will be your first and probably stiffest competition, especially if you are all calling on the same local accounts. Try to understand what services they are offering, and explain how your services will differ.

Next, be familiar with what operations that have a national or international footprint are doing. This includes Vistaprint, FedEx Office, the big box office superstores, UPS stores and the franchise chains. Some are offering more marketing services than others, but they are all moving that way. Finally, look outside your immediate geographic area if there are other areas that you are planning to serve. For example, if you have branches of national corporations in your back yard, be cognizant of the types of marketing services providers that might be located in the same general vicinity as their corporate headquarters. There are many instances of marketing services providers who have relationships locally and have been able to secure all or most of the national business due to their skills, capabilities and market differentiation.

For many of the competitors about which you will be seeking information, you can gain access to all or some of their pricing online, as well as details of what services they offer and how they are positioning themselves. Many also list key customers, which will give you an idea of which vertical markets they are focusing on.

Marketing Operations Management

This section is where you can describe the infrastructure you have, or plan to have, in place to support this new business. Your on-board marketing expert will be critical in creating this section. After all, as a marketing services provider, one of the key things you will be offering to marketers is the ability to streamline their operations. Questions to address include:

- What software will be in place to support the planning, managing, execution and measurement of the entire marketing system?

- What technology do you need to support needs for content management, digital asset management and collateral management?

- How will these systems be integrated to automate as much of the process as possible?

- How will you provide a marketing dashboard to your clients so that they can monitor campaign progress and other metrics that are important to them?

One approach is to acquire a number of point solutions and integrate them yourself. That can be easier today to the extent they are based on industry standards such as JDF or ISO 15076-1 for ICC specifications. Another approach is to look for a system that is already integrated, either self-contained (i.e., one application with a variety of integrated modules to accomplish certain specific activities and functions) or a system that is comprised of a number of point solutions but has already been integrated and proven by a trusted supplier.

Remember that according to the CMO Council, the top two objectives for marketers are streamlining their operations and providing better support for the sales organization. Demonstrating ROMI[22] is also critical to the success of marketers.

As you describe your marketing operations management approach, be sure to include people, process and technology. This includes an analysis of your current human resources, including skills gaps that need to be addressed in order for you to be successful in this new business venture. To help you with this effort, a sample skills assessment spreadsheet can be found at http://www.NewPathToProfit.com. For each position in your company you should develop a high-level job description that can be included in this section of the business plan.

TIP: Don't try to change the stripes on a zebra; assembling the right set of skills may require leopards and a move to spots instead of stripes.

Advertising and Promotion

The next thing to tackle is advertising and promotion—how are you going to get the word out about your new business? The first thing you need to do is build a campaign that tells people who you are, what you do, and what you can do to help their businesses. Walk the talk. Eat your own dog food. Maybe you partner with a marketing services

---

[22] Return on Marketing Investment

company for the first one, but since this is what you are selling to your customers, you need to be able to do it yourself. Use some of the more advanced techniques—personalized URLs, QR codes, social media—and make sure it is multi-touch. Include "old" media as well—newspapers, radio, even cable TV.

Most likely, you will want to target your local community, but you also want to target the vertical and/or horizontal markets in which you think you can be most successful, the ones you defined earlier in your business plan. The details of the campaign will be in your marketing plan, how you will execute. But in the business plan, you should describe the types of campaigns you will do, how often they will repeat, which channels you will use, how you will target your audiences. Of course, your marketing director will be an important part of this process.

By beginning the process with your own self-promotion, you will have more experience under your belt and will have an opportunity to refine your processes in a safe environment. Start small and branch out to a wider audience.

Think carefully about the creative, the messaging, the channels and the offer. Perhaps a grand opening celebration that features marketing-savvy speakers is the way to go. Or perhaps you can attract some new customers by offering a gift, drawing or some other incentive to get them to try you out. This will be an iterative process … you will need to estimate the costs of events or incentives to include in your business plan financials. Visit http://www.NewPathToProfit.com to view sample campaigns.

SWOT Analysis

Any good business plan will contain a SWOT analysis—what are your strengths, weaknesses (internal to the organization). What are the opportunities, threats (external to the organization). Be painfully honest when developing these.

Perhaps one strength is your existing customer base; and maybe you have had experience with a few campaigns with successful results. Perhaps you have strong working capital available, and reliable marketing management and support on your team, or strong business development skills. Weaknesses might include skills deficits among your people and some missing pieces in the technology infrastructure. Explain how you will leverage the strengths and mitigate the weaknesses. This is a great topic for you and your team to address in your off-site planning workshop.

Opportunities might include the fact that none of your local competitors are yet attempting this transformation. Or perhaps someone is going out of business and you have an opportunity to pick up a portfolio of new customers. Threats include the risk that marketers will not view you as credible. Or that one of the big players may be gearing up to enter your market. The rapid speed of technology change and the array of nontraditional competitors you will be facing should also go in the threats column. How will you take advantage of the opportunities, minimize the threats?

Historic Analysis

For your own edification, and for the information of anyone who may be looking at your business plan with an eye toward investing or partnering with you, you should include a historic analysis of your current business. The purpose of this section is to demonstrate that you know how to run a business, that you have good business acumen, and that history would indicate that you can pull this off.

Highlight any aspects of your current business that will help you in establishing the new one. Perhaps you have had experience with some campaigns for your company or your customers. Maybe you already have relationships or are dealing directly with some marketers in customer accounts.

You can also discuss your current competition here, and how making this transformation will give you even more competitive advantage. Make no mistake, there will be printer/mailer/fulfillment competitors you are staving off today who are trying to make these same moves. Much of what you discuss here will be applicable to your new business as well.

The following financial analyses can also be included in the historic analysis portion of the business plan:

- A three-year income statement for your current business
- A three-year balance sheet for your current business

Organizational Structure

This is an extremely important part of the business plan. In this section, you should describe how you are organized today, and what the organization will look like with the new business

- Are you simply adding new services to an existing portfolio of offerings, or are you starting up a new business under a different name?

- Where will the staffing come from? What percentage of your current staff will transition to the new business, and what condition does that leave the existing business in from a staffing perspective?

- Who will comprise your management team? At the risk of sounding like a broken record, a marketing professional should be part of that core team. But you also need finance, human resources, sales, operations, etc. Will you leverage some of those resources that are existing in the old business to serve the new, gaining synergies from sister companies?

Include organization charts from the current business and the proposed business. Appendix F has sample org charts from a mailing company, a fulfillment company and from a marketing services provider that you can compare, edit and use. Templates that you can use as a guide are also available online in the resource center for this book.

Your organizational plan should also contemplate the need to make changes over time as the business matures or the market changes.

TIP: Source your key marketing resource from an industry you are targeting, someone with 3 to 5 years working in that vertical market that can flop open a binder and show you how a campaign is planned, built, managed, executed and measured. If they can do those things and have 3 to 5 years of experience, that's an ideal candidate.

Contingency Planning

Of course, you can never anticipate all of the boulders that will make the path bumpy for this new business, but you should have a contingency plan to address common or foreseeable distress factors. For example, what happens when a key employee leaves the organization? Do you have any bench strength or how will you replace that person? Do you have a single customer who represents a significant percentage of your current business (not a good idea)? What happens if they defect or close? Think broadly and strategically about these issues.

One recommendation is to reach out to peer groups and look for others that have experience in these areas. Or you can work through an organization like the Mailing & Fulfillment Service Association (MFSA) that provides strong support; the association and many of its members are likely willing to share helpful strategies and tips with other businesses. There is a natural camaraderie in the industry, and most companies seem willing to help others become successful.

Marketing Services Provider Operations

The key in this section is to convey what will differentiate your company from others in the marketplace. You should have a crisp mission statement or elevator pitch developed that can articulate this. Take some advice from former Kodak CMO, Jeffrey Hayzlett. He suggests that you be able to tell someone what you do, concisely and distinctly, in 118 seconds. The time it takes to talk to someone in an elevator. Can you describe what you do in less than two minutes?

You should also address:

- Where the business will be located (marketing-oriented businesses are not particularly amenable to industrial locations).

- What type of premises will you be seeking? Will you have both businesses co-located, or will the new business be in an entirely different location? What are the pros and cons of each of those approaches?

- What will the office layout look like? You will need an inviting lobby, good conference room space, even guest offices where your clients can occasionally work. Production operations (printing, mailing, assembly,

Value Proposition

What is the value you are bringing to your customers that you will be promoting? Just as you want to bring new customers in from your own marketing campaign, that may be the value proposition you will focus on for customers. Others include customer retention, growing share of existing customers, reactivating former customers, tracking campaign results and delivering a measurable ROI, or even increasing brand awareness for the client. For each, describe how they are aligned with the business needs of the customer. For example, if customers are able to track the results of their campaigns, they will be able to determine which media deliver the best results or bring in the most qualified leads. They can then leverage the appropriate media to begin a dialog with qualified prospects that ultimately turns not only into sales, but into an ongoing and growing relationship.

Competitive Playing Field

Here you will express your market differentiation. You can draw on much of the work you have already done in your business plan, but focused on the execution aspect. How will your value proposition(s) be executed in a more efficient, cost effective, reliable, [you name the adjective] manner than the competition.

Company Strengths

Pulling from your SWOT analysis, delineate the strengths of your organization. Don't forget to mention that you have a captive or sister production operation (which differentiates you from most agencies) so that all of the work can be done under one roof.

Company Weaknesses

That captive production operation can also be a weakness. How many times have you heard, "My customers think of me as just a mail house." Describe how you will overcome weaknesses to gain the market position you are seeking. As we discussed earlier in the business plan, perhaps you will conduct a couple test self-promo campaigns that will cause your customers to begin looking at you differently.

[Year] Marketing Execution Plan

Remember that just sending out a newsletter or direct mailer without integrating it into a larger strategy will not deliver results. Especially in today's cluttered information environment, it takes multiple touches to make the sale.

According to David Shenk, author of *Data Smog, Surviving the Information Glut*, consumers encounter up to 3,000 marketing messages a day! Where do you think your one newsletter each month will end up in someone's pile? While it may get noticed, it certainly is competing with other messages. Thus, to increase the chances that people will take action on what we send, we must reach out to them multiple times, in multiple ways, using multiple media.

ProspectZone.com recommends seven to ten touches to effectively help a prospect make the connection between your company and the business problems you can help them solve. When that happens, you have greatly increased your chances of making a sale.

Those touches are most effective when using multiple channels, media, and response methods but with a consistent theme that builds recognition and awareness among recipients. Similar messages and themes are also used across all media, such as your postcard, the web landing page or the email that follows up the direct mail flyer. Each has the same creative feel and messaging. This is Cross-Media!

Also like the business plan, this is a living, breathing document that should be frequently revisited to see how you are doing against objectives, and refined as needed. You will make mistakes. That is a given. But you will learn from those mistakes and move on. Managing and monitoring the marketing plan is a full-time job and cannot be squeezed into the many tasks your current team has on their respective plates just keeping up with the day-to-day business. Yes, you are right. Once again, I am going to emphasize the importance of having a dedicated marketing professional on your team BEFORE you begin writing the business and marketing plans. This professional will also be a boon to your sales efforts, bringing you credibility with marketers as you work through your transformation.

Here are some of the tactical items you can include in your marketing plan. I am sure you and your team will be able to come up with many others; this is just a starting point.

- Send out hard copy/e-newsletter every quarter
- Campaign to collect email addresses for eNewsletter signup

- eNewsletter one-pager sent every month (need a writer)
- Postcard with personalized URL every other month to verticals with A/B testing
- Whitepapers, two per year
- Blog Posts—how frequently? If entries are not kept current and interesting, no one will visit. Who will write it?
- Case Studies (Write a short story about every customer win. If you don't have permission to use the customer name, work around that. These can be placed in inventory and used for blogs, press releases, on your web site and in sales efforts.)
- Thought-leader one pagers, such as "What can QR codes do for you?"
- Run Holiday promotions (July and Dec)
- Reach out to various online and/or printed magazines that your prospects read
- Social Media outreach on LinkedIn, Twitter, and Facebook at a minimum. Again, these must show a decent level of activity and stay current.
- YouTube videos of case studies (customer testimonials)
- Host an educational seminar

These tactics should be mapped out on a monthly basis with budgets. A spreadsheet that will help you get this going is included—guess where?—in the online resource center for this book. An example is shown in Figure 13.

Figure 13. Example Calendar of Marketing Tactics

Jan	1_____2_____3_____			Jul	1_____2_____3_____		
Feb	1_____2_____3_____			Aug	1_____2_____3_____		
Mar	1_____2_____3_____			Sep	1_____2_____3_____		
Apr	1_____2_____3_____			Oct	1_____2_____3_____		
May	1_____2_____3_____			Nov	1_____2_____3_____		
Jun	1_____2_____3_____			Dec	1_____2_____3_____		

Future Plans to Keep In Mind:
- X
- y

That's it. You're done. For the moment, anyway. You have your business plan and marketing plan in place. You will be revisiting your business plan at least annually, and your marketing plan will become the playbook for your on-staff marketing professional.

Business Transformation Timeline

You should be congratulating yourself on progress made, but don't get too excited yet! With the business and marketing plans in place, the work is just beginning. Figure 14 is a business transformation timeline. Across the top are the various services you might implement; across the bottom is the education process you must undergo to get there successfully. You can construct your own timeline, including dates, to help you measure your progress along the transformation path.

Figure 14. Business Transformation Timeline

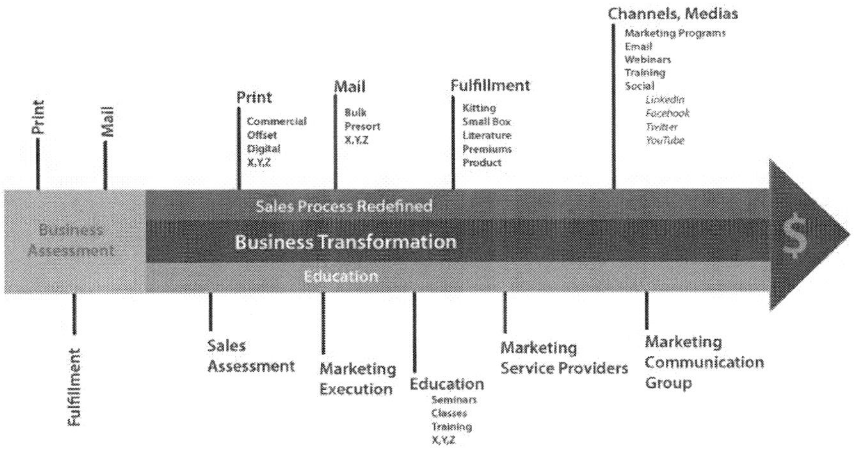

In this example, the transformation begins with the first phase—business assessment—knowing that you are still doing a lot of print, mail and fulfillment, which are your legacy or traditional services. As you move along the timeline, gaining more knowledge, you add more services, until ultimately you have reached the point when you can step back and say, "We really are a marketing services provider!" This will mean that you have diversified the services that you offer, and the channels that you are helping people with are more balanced, as opposed to solely relying on print, mail, and fulfillment.

It is the real world, however, and there actually is no end to the transformation. You can be guaranteed that things will change again. But you will reach a point where you are very comfortable with the way the business is going and the value you are delivering to customers, ready to take on the next challenge. You likely will still be producing standalone direct mail projects, but you will also be comfortable with email, viral tell-a-friend campaigns, QR codes, personalized URLs, electronic newsletters, social media, and more. To look at this from a different perspective, look at the chart from Winterberry in this book – it lists components of the marketing supply chain that make up the value of the marketing department.

I will leave you with this thought as we conclude Chapter Four. People say to me all the time, "Wow, this is overwhelming, John, or it seems overwhelming." My response is, "Reality check time: It is not easy. That's why we wrote the book. Fundamentally, we think that with strategy and plans, you have a better chance of success. If the people that buy your products today are there—needing these services—how can you not be there to help them?" Whenever we sell or market a product or service based on the needs and affinities of our target audience, we need to be there with them in a way that is measurable, helping our customers get their customers through the lead generation funnel.

Next we will discuss the required infrastructure—people, process, technology—in more detail in Chapter Five.

Keys to Success

- This transformation should be approached as though you

were starting a new business—which, in essence, you are.

- A solid business plan boosts your credibility and also provides lenders with the information needed to make a funding decision.

- Without marketing expertise on staff, it will be difficult—if not impossible—to transform your business and build credibility with your customers.

- The downside of transformation is that establishing a new business can be scary, especially in an uncertain economy. But the good news is that you already have an ongoing business and existing customers that can help fund this new venture.

- In an off-site team workshop, examine the trends affecting your prospective customer base. This includes trends specific to individual vertical markets you may wish to target, as well as horizontal trends.

- As you build your new infrastructure to support your business transformation—in people, processes and technology—your goal should be to establish a clear offering that encompasses capabilities that may be just out of reach for many marketers.

- You should also set expectations for your team that this transformation will not happen overnight, and it will not be easy. It will take the full dedication of the entire team to make the transformation successful. And it will take leadership from you to galvanize the organization.

- There is no end to the need to review and update marketing strategies; it is an area that is always evolving and changing, and it needs constant reflection and review to ensure that it stays current with changing market needs.

- Offering marketing services is very different from buying new production equipment, however. The analytics are not always as clear-cut. Each service must be a line item in the business plan and in the pro forma financials.

- By beginning marketing services transformation with your own self-promotion, you will have more experience under

Figure 15. Anatomy of an Integrated Campaign

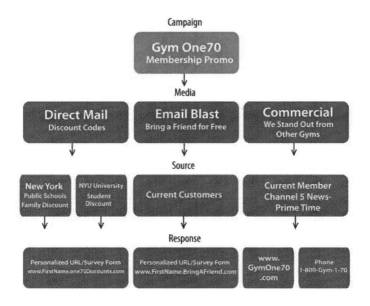

Some of the difficulty that mailing & fulfillment businesses have had in achieving a successful transformation is actually bigger than not understanding marketing. It requires a "back to basics" approach and a new business mentality that asks, "What do I need to do to change my business?" The value-based sales approach is critical.

Figure 16 presents another way of mapping out a campaign. In this case, it starts with a specific goal—to increase sales by 15%. The media are identified—direct mail and email. And then the target audiences are segmented. For purchased lists, the mailer includes a Business Reply Card (BRC). There is typically less information available about the recipients from a purchased list than about previous buyers. In this example, previous buyers are offered two response mechanisms, a personalized URL or the call center. Newsletter subscribers are already receiving email newsletters from the client and can easily click through to a web registration page. If email addresses are available for previous buyers, they are good candidates for receiving an email promotion as well.

Figure 16. Alternative Campaign Flow Chart

Whenever you execute a marketing campaign, remember this. A marketing campaign has no end. That is right, it has no end. You will always have non respondents to reach out to. There will always be more information you can gather about your prospects. There will always be people who you converted that may want something more. Always take what you learned and the information you gained the first time, then refine and re-launch. This is known as "actionable intelligence," which means you are gaining information you can then use in your next efforts.

What happens when it's all done? Well, that's another part of wearing a marketing hat—determining what happens next! Use the reporting on a campaign like the one above to learn what worked and what did not work. Refine those steps, and then execute the next campaign. You can drive recurring business by utilizing the intelligence that you've gained from each previous campaign.

Figure 17 illustrates this. Use the data that you have available in the marketing reports and dashboard to get the next campaign started.

Figure 17. Building Recurring Revenues Based on Actionable Intelligence

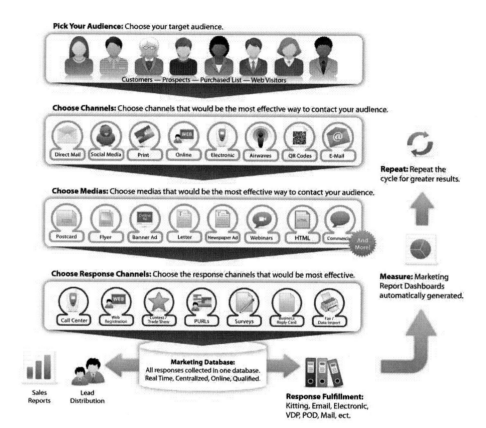

Putting the Pieces Together

In a promotion such as the gym promotion, the technology infrastructure must include the ability to execute direct mail and email campaigns with personalized URLs, as well as the ability to create and place a TV commercial. Not all of this must be internal; for example, a marketing services provider might partner with an ad agency to handle the TV commercial part of the campaign. Call center activity might also be outsourced. But the ability to do your own direct mail (including printing) and email production and distribution in-house is a highly desirable piece of the infrastructure. It gives you control over the campaign, the ability to track responses, and a demonstrated value for your services to the customer. It also keeps costs down (and margins up). Once you have the infrastructure in place, it can be reused across many campaigns, making these investments easier to justify.

If you are committed to this transformation, these are the table stakes—the minimum requirements to get in the game. From that point, other media can be snapped in as new options and customer requirements arise. But again, all investments must be made with the future vision of a completely integrated solution.

I spoke to a firm in Iowa who executed a multi-channel campaign that utilized channels that were a bit out of its traditional scope of business. The company pushed out direct mail pieces to a million+ people that had multiple calls to action:

- Personalized URLs
- Call Center
- Business Reply Cards

The firm was able to easily set up the personalized URLs and landing pages. However, this campaign required extended capabilities to also execute and measure Call Center responses and Business Reply Cards. The firm partnered with a company to manage and record the Call Center activity and used local resources to input the data from Business Reply Cards.

Even though this company used partners to execute this large campaign, it recognized the importance of demonstrating to its client that it was a full-services marketing solutions provider. Data from all three response mechanisms was entered into one system. Thus, the client could view all leads through one dashboard.

The Digital Highway

As your marketing services business grows, so will the amount of electronic traffic in and out of your business. This means you must be sure you have an adequate and scalable pipeline that can handle the volume. This includes connections to the outside world, as well as your internal network, servers and storage capability. Some of the requirement can be offloaded if you are using Software as a Service for all or some of the pieces, as long as you ensure that the provider has an adequate set-up and appears to have a reasonably long-term viability. You can also leverage cloud computing[23], which is gaining steam in the marketplace.

Business Continuity and Security

As you will be handling customer data, you also must ensure that you have full disaster recovery and business continuity plans in place, as well as to ensure full security of customer data. This will be one of the first questions you are asked as customers begin to investigate placing their marketing campaigns with you, and you should be fully prepared to explicitly, confidently and accurately explain your process and the precautions you will take to protect their data. This is not a subject you can dance around. You need to have it covered.

If you are using a Software as a Service or cloud computing provider, do your homework to make sure the provider can guarantee business continuity and security for you and your customers and has a plan in place to migrate usable data back to you should they experience business difficulties.

TIP: Consider creating a written document that fully outlines your business continuity and security plan. This can be posted on your web site for downloading and/or used as a customer leave-behind. If it is well done, it will increase your credibility immeasurably.

---

[23] From Wikipedia, June 2011: Cloud computing refers to the use and access of multiple server-based computational resources via a digital network (WAN, Internet connection using the World Wide Web, etc.). Cloud users may access the server resources using a computer, netbook, pad computer, smart phone, or other device. In cloud computing, applications are provided and managed by the cloud server and data is also stored remotely in the cloud configuration. Users do not download and install applications on their own device or computer; all processing and storage is maintained by the cloud server. The on-line services may be offered from a cloud provider or by a private organization.

Tools of the Trade

Ensure that your employees are equipped with computers that are up to date, have sufficient power for the tasks that are expected of them, and have the necessary software to function effectively. Keep all desktop hardware and software at the current release. This is not a place to skimp!

Production

Obviously, you will need to assess your production platform. If you have printing capabilities in place, re your presses up to the challenge in terms of quality, productivity and throughput? If you don't have presses and cannot or do not want to make that investment early on, can you find a nearby partner who has extra capacity and is willing to work closely with you? This approach has worked well for years for many mailing operations. A cautionary note, however: Just as you may be considering adding printing, many printers are adding mailing and fulfillment. Choose your partner with care and give serious consideration to bringing printing services in house if you haven't already done so.

What about inserters and other production equipment? How up to date is your fulfillment platform, and how easily can it scale? What are you doing about envelopes? Does it make sense to print—if not convert—them yourself? What type of inkjet systems do you have in place for application of variable data? Do they support full color? What is the age of the various equipment components you have on the floor? Are they relatively new and equipped with the latest upgrades and productivity features? There is a need for speed in this new business. Don't let your aging production equipment be the bottleneck. Keep in mind that most types of production equipment have both an operational life and a market life. The tendency is to keep, for example, an operational long beyond its market life; it is paid for, right? This is almost always a bad decision, whether you are making the transformation to marketing services provider or not. If you do have aged equipment, could it use a coat of paint? Customers conducting a plant visit can be put off by tacky, tattered equipment on the floor, even if it operates perfectly.

If you do not have offset presses and need them in the mix—not everyone will—find a reliable outsource partner or consider investing in an automated direct imaging offset press such as the Presstek DI.

These presses come in a variety of sizes and some can be expanded up to 10 colors. Their high level of automation and relatively small footprint means they can more easily be placed in environments that have not previously had offset presses.

It's Not Finished Till It's Finished

Don't forget about bindery and fulfillment. Inline finishing is ideal for many applications; nearline finishing should be as automated as possible, using the JDF standard to automate setup. Do you have or need die cutting and other specialized equipment? Mailing, shipping or other distribution and fulfillment processes should also be as streamlined as possible. This will take time, error and much of the potential need for rework out of the process.

Tying It All Together

Finally, do you own an MIS solution? If so, have you fully implemented it and do you keep it current? A good MIS implementation affects virtually every employee in the company. It is the heartbeat of the operation. It provides you with real-time business and production data that allows you to effectively run the business. As an increasing number of suppliers are working to deliver JDF-compliant solutions to the market, an MIS system is the key to entering data only once, or having it automatically entered into the system by the processes and equipment themselves. Running a business at the speed of the Internet, which is what marketing services providers must do, requires a solid MIS solution. It is the only way you will be able to keep tabs on everything that is going on within your company, and to move work through the process smoothly. Implementing an MIS solution is not trivial, but it will pay for itself in the long run.

The Right People

People are undoubtedly one of the most important investments. Without the right people in place, no business functions well.

> *"In the end, an organization is nothing more than the collective capacity of its people to create value."*

Lou Gerstner (1942-) former Chairman & CEO of IBM

Marketing

At the risk of being redundant, I will say again that the most important "people acquisition" you need to make in this transformation is a marketing professional. This has already been discussed at length, but bears repeating here.

Sales

As several of the case studies in this book pointed out, the next big challenge is sales. Business owners who have begun selling marketing services typically tell us that a small percentage of their existing sales people will make the trip. To the extent they are willing and able to learn a new way of selling, they will find selling marketing services to be challenging but rewarding. If they are not willing or able to make the transition, keep in mind that there is still a legacy business that must be maintained to fund development of the new business. Your best sales people will also have critical customer relationships that can be mined for new business. I want to be perfectly clear that I am not suggesting that you fire sales reps that are bringing you in $3 million a year in traditional business. You still need those sales reps. They sustain what you have. They may never turn into your star marketing solutions sales folks, but they clearly have an important role. That being said, you do want to have people on your staff that can talk the new talk, and walk the new walk.

Solution selling is different than selling coffee beans or business cards! There are many sources about solution selling for you to review. I recommend a couple of books in Appendix H, and http://www.NewPathToProfit.com also has sales-oriented resources for you.

The bottom line is that more than likely you will need to add at least one new solutions sales person. In many companies, the traditional sales force is tasked with uncovering opportunities and making introductions, and the solutions sales specialist is then engaged to help structure the deal. The solutions sales specialist should also be tasked with calling on marketing folks at new accounts. The sales process will be addressed in more detail in Chapter Eight.

If you don't want to wait for Chapter 8, we have a free resource for you. Scan the QR Code below to download interlinkONE's free eBook, "Guide to Selling Marketing Services":

Information Technology

If you don't already have an IT department, one should be established. Sometimes these technical folks can be very valuable on sales calls, as they can more quickly ferret out customer requirements and map them to company capabilities. Sometimes they work in the background on implementation. Or both. While you do want to be able to replicate your offerings across multiple customers, each customer will almost always have some unique requirements. Most software providers offer professional services, and you could choose to take advantage of those services for any required customizations. But to the extent you can have at least some of this capability in house, your operation will be more efficient.

The other side of the IT coin is the need to make sure that all IT and network systems are maintained and running well, just as you do with your production equipment. You may be able to source this person (or persons) from inside the organization. But more than likely, you will need to go outside to find the appropriate resource.

Rounding It Out

Clearly, you need the best possible operations and production people on the job across all parts of the operation, as well as the normal roles of accounting, HR, etc. The skills assessment tool that can be downloaded from this book's web resource page will help in identifying the skills required by job type, both in assessing your current staff and in assisting with the hiring process.

Bench Strength

It is also wise to have some bench strength—talented people you can groom for potential future openings. You may find these people as you interact with other businesses. They could be summer interns. Or you may want to recruit new graduates for a training program. Some leading companies I have spoken with routinely hire new graduates, rotating them through an organized training program that touches every department. If managed correctly, this benefits both the employee and the company, and can be the equivalent of earning a Master's degree!

There are a number of colleges that provide a tremendous amount of business communications related knowledge to their students. This includes Rochester Institute of Technology (RIT), Clemson University, Cal-Poly and more. Service providers can greatly improve their chances of success by reaching out to and bringing employees from these schools onto their workforce.

Process

Since we have just been speaking about people, a key process that you need to ensure is working well is hiring and retaining good employees. All too often, these important assets are not managed as effectively as they could be, ultimately reducing the overall value of the company and its ability to compete effectively. Human resources management practices in graphics communications companies are often reactive rather than proactive, resulting in less-than-optimum hires and poor employee retention. A rotating door of employees in and out is not only disruptive, but it is expensive as well, and can have a negative effect on morale and on customer perception. Make sure you have a strong HR process in place, including both hiring and employee retention. You should have some type of career path in place that even the least skilled employees can take advantage of if they have the will and are willing to undergo training. Some companies even make online training available to employees on-site that they can take advantage of outside of working hours to gain certifications in various disciplines.

Lean, Green and Mean

Have you educated yourself about the principles of lean manufacturing? If not, now is a good time to do so.[24] By following the principles of lean manufacturing, you will be able to find and demolish waste in both time and materials. Most companies who have gone

---

[24] The IPA/IDEAlliance (www.IPA.org) has an affordable graphic-arts-specific online e-LEAN program that can be perused at your convenience and shared with appropriate employees.

through a lean manufacturing assessment are startled to learn how much waste there is in their operating processes.

An optimum manufacturing process built on the principles of lean manufacturing will also be more environmentally sustainable. Beyond that, take a look at your building, energy consumption, recycling processes and the materials you use in manufacturing, including paper, chemistry and more, to find opportunities to make your business greener. Green is good for Mother Earth, but it is also good for business. For example, how much energy (and cost) can you save by changing light bulbs from incandescent to fluorescent? What happens to soda cans and bottles, and other recylables employees have access to on site or bring to work with them? One company put an aggressive office waste recyling program into effect, allowing the employees to use the proceeds for employee events, such as "Pizza Friday's." This can be a strong incentive for employees to get on the green bandwagon.

Once you have considered these things—lean manufacturing and environmental sustainability—you will find ways to streamline your organization, and truly be lean, green and mean.

Production Automation

We have already discussed the importance of buying and implementing JDF-compliant solutions. There are so many ways this will streamline your operation as you begin to let machines and processes communicate bi-directionally with each other. Even something a simple as implementing an electronic job ticket to give all employees real-time access to job information without the need to run around looking for the paper copy will make an amazing difference in the speed at which jobs can move through your plant. The objective is to remove as many touches as possible from each and every job. Perhaps you will never reach the level of automation that exists at Vistaprint—no more than 60 seconds of human intervention for each job—but you will almost always find room for improvement.

Relentlessly pursuing automation and efficiency is ongoing and vigilance is required to ensure that every bit of waste possible is ruthlessly stripped from the operation.

A Fundamental Shift

People, process and technology: It all adds up to a fundamental shift in the way you do business, from a job-oriented transactional business process to selling, delivering, consulting and reporting on integrated business solutions. These infrastructure considerations will help you to ensure you have the right pieces in place to make that fundamental shift.

Cash Flow

All of these things require investments, and the importance of a business plan that generates enough cash flow cannot be underestimated. The recent recession and the devastating effect it had on businesses that were overleveraged highlight the importance of careful and thoughtful planning of investments. As part of your business plan, you should have projected cash flow figures that are based on a conservative yet realistic view of how many of these new services you can expect to sell and what resources it will take to get your business in shape to sell them. With a good understanding of cash flow, you will be able to identify the cash going in and out of your business in respect to sales and all expenses. It also allows you to project ahead and make adjustments so you can see what is happening and fine tune along the way.

When I started my business in 1996, I found that the proforma financials including cash flow really helped to identify a number of things. What kind of capital do I need to make this business run? What I am going to sell? How much I am going to sell it for? Good and honest answers to those questions are critical for marketing services providers making the transformation.

I am always surprised when I get calls from folks asking me how much they should charge for certain services. This is a clear indicator that the business plan was not done right or perhaps not done at all, and that if they do have a plan in place, they are not revisiting it as new opportunities arise.

> **TIP:** *The basic question that needs to be asked and answered is: What price will I establish for each service and how many do I need to sell to make the business viable?*

One item you will be selling is marketing campaign services. A marketing campaign could include everything from direct mail to email to seminars or events. When you sell the entire solution, you are doing just that—not selling each component individually. Within the campaign, there might be data management, there might be some print, some mail, some electronic media, some kitting & fulfillment, or even television advertising as in our gym example earlier. It might include Twitter or other social media. You need to be able to bundle that price, keeping in mind the cost of all of the human and other resources required for execution of the campaign. In the figure below, you can see an example of what might be involved in the production and promotion of a seminar. How much of this business are you getting, or offering to your clients? How much are you leaving on the table?

Figure 18. Sample Multi-Channel Campaign

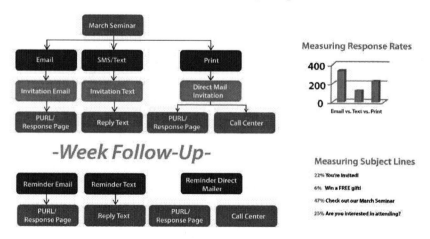

Sure, each campaign will be different, but for purposes of cash flow planning, your offering needs to be well-defined enough to allow you to build an estimated average cost and selling price for a set number of campaign types. This can be expanded and adjusted as you gain more experience, but start small to keep it manageable. Your marketing professional will be of great value here.

This is different from the budgeted hourly rates you probably already have established for equipment and other cost centers within your plant. It is a bundled program. And as I have emphasized before, it is not the cost-plus pricing you may be used to; it is value-based pricing. What is the value to the customer and what is a reasonable profit you should be able to achieve for delivering that value?

In comparing this approach to the typical approach in a printing, mailing or fulfillment business, I like to use this analogy. If a customer opportunity comes along that requires purchase of a new piece of equipment, these business executives are very, very good at determining that selling this new product to a particular target market will require a certain piece of equipment. It will need someone on the equipment to pull the handles and push the buttons. It will consume a certain amount of overhead. And it will require resources to actually sell the output. What I am suggesting is a broader perspective on the nature of the product being sold that reaches back into the customer organization to determine the benefits the customer can achieve. For example, can an administrative position or two be eliminated or the people reassigned to more productive tasks if you can manage all of the organization's literature fulfillment through an online storefront? That's part of the value you bring to the customer and part of the entire program. The business owners that understand this early in the process are typically much more successful with the transformation.

If you are looking for an expert on the subject of cash flow, capital investments, and other economic-related news for the graphic communications industry, we'd like to recommend checking out NAPL's Andrew Paparozzi, Vice President/Chief Economist. Visit NAPL's website for a frequently updated blog at: http://ilink.me/NAPLblogs. You can also follow WhatTheyThink's Dr. Joe Webb, Director of the Economics & Research Center at WhatTheyThink.com/ERC or Twitter - http://www.twitter.com/wtterc

Building For Success

This chapter contains valuable insight and advice that will help you put the right building blocks for success into place. In Chapter Six, we build on those blocks, moving on to how to be the best marketing services provider ever.

Keys to Success

- With the business and marketing plan under your belt and a marketing expert on staff, the next step in your transformation that requires your attention is your infrastructure.

- A successful transformation requires taking a broader view, and having a plan in place before acquiring any new hardware or software.

- A campaign is not a slice or a one-time, one-media contact; it is an entire program.

- As your marketing services business grows, so will the amount of electronic traffic in and out of your business. This means you must be sure you have an adequate and scalable pipeline that can handle the volume.

- As you will be handling customer data, you also must ensure that you have full disaster recovery and business continuity plans in place, as well as to ensure full security of customer data.

- Ensure that your employees are equipped with computers that are up to date, have sufficient power for the tasks that are expected of them, and have the necessary software to function effectively.

- Running a business at the speed of the Internet, which is

what marketing services providers must do, requires a solid MIS solution

- Business owners who have begun selling marketing services typically tell us that two in ten of their existing print sales people will make the trip.

- It is wise to have some bench strength—talented people you can groom for potential future openings.

- Have you educated yourself about the principles of lean manufacturing? If not, now is a good time to do so.

- Relentlessly pursuing automation and efficiency is ongoing and vigilance is required to ensure that every bit of waste possible is stripped from the operation.

- As part of your business plan, you should have projected cash flow figures that are based on a conservative yet realistic view of how many of these new services you can expect to sell and what resources will take to get your business in shape to sell them.

Okay, maybe you aren't aiming to win an award for being the best marketing services provider. But you definitely want your clients raving about you and your services. You want them to refer your new business. You want the satisfaction of clients who thank you profusely after a really awesome marketing campaign. And we know marketing services providers for whom all of these things ring true. Not only are they getting kudos from their customers for making a difference in their bottom line, but they are also seeing significant bottom line benefits of their own—and growth, even in a tough economy.

In order to reach that stage, it is important to build the right types of activities into your business and your own personal business day in order to ensure that you can provide top-notch services on an ongoing basis and keep 'em coming back for more.

This chapter presents five best practices that any marketing services provider can benefit from. Each and every one will spur your business to even greater success. All of these things take time, and your days are probably already way too hectic. Find ways to delegate more to your stellar staff in order to make time for you to be the thought leader they need to take them through the balance of this journey. You and your business will benefit. And your employees will benefit and grow as well, especially as you begin demonstrating even more confidence in their abilities to take on new and challenging assignments as you lead them into the future.

1 – Stay well-read and educated.

While you certainly don't need to know everything about marketing, technology, social media and the like, there is no free pass. If you want your business to be successful, you must take the time to stay current with the trends and happenings that affect the marketplace. Whether it is new technology, new communications platforms, new developments in mobile communications, or even something as seemingly esoteric as Amazon's new tablet computer, a purported competitor to Apple's iPad, you must keep yourself informed. Believe me, your customers make time to do these things. And when you call on them, you will want to be able to discuss trends and issues with them knowledgeably as well—taking the conversation to the next level relative to how new developments position you to add even more value for your customers.

What publications are your clients reading? What web sites do they regularly visit? If you don't know, you need to find out, because you should be keeping an eye on the information that is important to them. What associations do they belong to? What trade shows do they attend? What books are they reading? All of these will give you much more than topics for cocktail party conversations. It will increase your knowledge and your credibility. It will position you to say to your customers, "I know the challenges that are facing you, and I know how I can help."

You should also stay on top of marketing and business basics by reading blogs, newsletters and other publications with the latest information. If you find a good blogger, you can subscribe to be notified when something new is posted. For example, you might want to visit Tamar Weinberg's Techipedia.com to hear what this social media expert has to say about the social media realm. Seth Godin always has something interesting and relevant to say in his blog, ThisIsSethsBlog, as well as through his Domino Project initiative designed to change the way books come to market. Or perhaps you want to keep tabs on the latest printing industry news through several blogs accessible from WhatTheyThink's home page. One way I have found to stay on top of relevant topics is to use Google Reader; you can select from a variety of sources to receive up-to-the-minute news and updates. It is a convenient way to sort through the news, reading the items that catch your interest. Using this method, you will often become exposed to ideas that you normally might not have come across reading the newspaper or watching CNN.

Another option to help you stumble upon great resources is StumbleUpon.com. Once you set up a free account, you will be amazed at the useful information you can find. A simple search for marketing turned up more than a half million hits, ranging from the free online encyclopedia Wikipedia to MarketingProfs and Marketing Mogul. Chapter Nine has more detailed information on the social media scene that will also give you many ideas about places to look to keep your knowledge up to date.

This is not about information overload. It's about staying on top of things that are happening that affect your business and your target market(s). It's about using today's technology to stay tuned into what's hot and what's not.

Appendix H has a suggested reading list of my favorite books. I am sure you will be able to add many more to your list. And while you are at it, share your favorites with your staff to keep them interested and excited as well.

TIP: *Want to stay informed online?* *Use Google Alerts to monitor specific terms or phrases to see what people are saying about it. Keep up on the latest news from important customers and prospects. It continuously scans web for relevant stories and delivers updates to your email address or to a window in your Google Desktop Sidebar.*

2 – Be forward-thinking.

While you're staying on top of the game (see #1 above), you should always be thinking about how you can make things work for the future. How can you use technology or information in the near- (and long-) term to better position your business and help your clients. *Status quo* (AKA "the same ol' way of thinking" or "business as usual") should no longer be your mindset. It's all about taking what you know and using it to think up ways to work better, faster, more efficiently in the future. It is about innovation and entrepreneurship. It is about the spark of an idea you get when reading your favorite blogger or publication, a news item, or a new book and growing that into a bonfire of a great new business idea.

Take notes in your books, write things down as you think of them, conduct brainstorming sessions with your employees, take the time to listen to a few of the multitude of free or fee webinars being offered. Be curious. You never know when you will stumble upon the next greatest-ever business idea that can propel you and your customers to an even more profitable future.

You also want to find ways to visually demonstrate to your clients that you are a forward-thinker. Sure, some situations may require that you take notes. But why not bring your iPad with you to business meetings? Demonstrate that you have and use new technology. Not only will this help start conversations, it will position you as someone that is moving forward.(And the iPad is a great way to be prepared for snappy on-the-fly demos or presentations!)

Understand what is next in the world of marketing services. New channels will emerge, and marketing departments will certainly become curious, and want to investigate whether they can use them to reach prospects and customers. If you look ahead like they do, you will be able to provide help when they need it.

TIP: Check out http://ilnk.me/tools, a convenient collection of tools and strategies you can use to generate profitable ideas and capitalize on the opportunities available in the new global economy.

3 – Be aggressive.

This is not the time to sit back and relax. Yes, you've made the decision to transform your business into a marketing services provider model. And that's great. But the ambition shouldn't stop there. You should be thinking aggressively about how to further build your business and your client base going forward. How can you woo those prospects and make them fall in love with your business? How can you ensure that existing customers will always wonder how they ever got along without you? How can you make your competitors sit up and take notice—yet stay miles ahead of them as you develop new and innovative products and services?

Thomas Edison once said, "Opportunity is missed by most people because it is dressed in overalls and looks like work." Yes, making the jump to offering marketing services may not be the prettiest or easiest undertaking of your career. But being willing to work hard and be aggressive will help you find success.

> ***TIP: 10 Ways to Stay Ahead of the Competition from The Business Insider:*** http://ilnk.me/StayAhead

4 – Be prepared.

Clients will begin to expect certain services and support from you as a marketing services provider. You can't just offer personalized URLs and think you're set for the foreseeable future. You need to prepare yourself to offer a full range of multichannel marketing services and to add new channels at the drop of a hat, as they become viable or of interest to your client base. You must have the solutions in place that allow you to support the work that your clients will be tapping you for (or *want to*). You need to prepare for the day when you truly become a one-stop marketing services shop. Being prepared from the get-go will set your business up for a successful future.

> ***TIP: It is better to be prepared for an opportunity and not have one than to have an opportunity and not be prepared.*** **(Whitney M. Young, Jr.)**

One way to be prepared for opportunities is to diversify by adding services that you know your customers are using from other sources, or that they have been asking you for. If one customer is looking to you for a particular service, it is likely that others will as well.

Diversification of your business can make you stronger and more attractive to customers. Consider diversifying your business to be better prepared to meet emerging customer needs by:

- Vertically integrating: this refers to integrating your business along the value chain, both upstream and downstream, so that each link in the value chain efficiently feeds the others. By making the decision to become a marketing services provider, you are already going down this path, extending your reach upstream and downstream in the marketing value chain.

Perhaps adding creative services is an opportunity for you in this new realm of marketing services. This is an area where you can start small and grow. It is a great opportunity to bring in a graphic design intern or hire a new graduate.

What about adding or updating your printing capabilities? Many customers would prefer to have printing, mailing and fulfillment under a single roof. You can be sure that printing houses are looking to add mailing and fulfillment ... why not the other way around?

• Horizontal diversification: move into new or related industries. This could mean adding promotional items, logo'd apparel, video services or access to other products and services tangentially related to what you do today. If you have a robust online storefront, you can easily link to other providers of these services, taking a cut of each sale without the need to make a big investment.

• Geographic diversification: The beauty of the Internet is that it levels the playing field and removes geographic barriers. While once you may have been a local or regional service provider, as you move into the realm of marketing services, take the opportunity to expand your geographic reach. This becomes even more viable as you begin to add printing services to the mix, eliminating the need for customers to ship printed materials long distances to your shop for mailing & fulfillment. You can expand geographically be by supporting regional offices of locally-headquartered companies you are already serving. Or you may choose to focus on particular vertical markets, such as banks or retail, expanding your reach to companies in these industries located in different geographies.

Being prepared is being ready for anything. Are you ready for anything?

> *TIP: Don't fall back on commodity comfort. Ensure that your focus is on providing solutions to your clients.*

5 – "Walk the Talk."

Talking will only take you so far. You need to back up what you say with actions. At the end of the day, even the smoothest sales person still needs to be able to implement the stuff his company is selling. In order to be a top-notch marketing services provider, you must use your own solutions to create self-promotional marketing campaigns. This allows you to reach your prospects with the same tools you will be trying to sell to them. Pretty ingenious, while at the same time, quite basic. It requires an agency mindset, a marketer's mindset. Can you offer these services? Can you effectively use them to promote your own business? We will discuss self-promotion in more detail in the next chapter.

Walking the talk is a must-do for success in the marketing services business. Your business and marketing plans should lay out how you will be doing this, the resources that are required, and the metrics against which you will measure your success. These are exactly the services you are proposing to offer your customers as a marketing services provider. If you can't use them for your own business purposes, what basis will you have to convince customers they can be used effectively for theirs? If you are recommending integrated marketing campaigns to your customers, your own case studies can be a great starting place. If you plan to help customers with social media or search engine optimization (SEO), how do your efforts stack up? These are all important questions you must ask—and answer—as you start this journey.

> *TIP: 10 Best Interactive Marketing Practices from iMedia Connection* **http://ilnk.me/10best**

Keys to Success

- Stay well-read and educated. If you want your business to be successful, you must take the time to stay current with the trends and happenings that affect the marketplace.

- Be forward-thinking. How can you use technology or information in the near- (and long-) term to better position your business and help your clients.

- Be aggressive. This is not the time to sit back and relax.

- Be prepared. You need to prepare yourself to offer a full range of multichannel marketing services and to add new channels at the drop of a hat as they become viable or of interest to your client base.

- Diversification of your business can make you stronger and more attractive to customers. Consider diversifying your business to be better prepared to meet emerging customer needs.

- Walk the Talk. In order to be a top-notch marketing services provider, you must use your own solutions to create self-promotional marketing campaigns.

CHAPTER SEVEN

WALKING THE TALK—HOW TO PROMOTE THE HECK OUT OF YOUR NEW BUSINESS

The Right Portfolio at the Right Time

With all of the technologies out there and all the fancy-schmancy words that describe them, it's easy to get side-tracked and think that everything you knew about marketing in the traditional sense is wrong. In fact, we can't emphasize enough that it's important not to throw all that you know out the window. You know why? Because traditional marketing still works!! Marketing fundamentals are just that—fundamentals. They don't change a whole lot.

What has changed, however, is that technology has opened up a whole new world for you to use when you market. Technology has truly changed the game in terms of new ways to reach prospects, new ways to send messages, new ways for your prospects to respond. And you can measure it all…so you know what's working and what's not.

You are probably doing a certain amount of marketing already. But maybe some people would term it "old school." You surely have a Yellow Pages ad. Perhaps you mail out flyers or occasionally put an ad in the newspaper or on local TV. You probably have a web site, and maybe you have done some Search Engine Optimization (SEO) to improve the ability of customers and prospects to find you.

But these things, while still valuable, are not sufficient. They are a transactional approach to the business. They are not designed to establish a dialog with your customers and prospects. They are a one-time hit, in most cases, and not the type of product you will be selling as a marketing services provider.

TIP: *Your web site can often be the first interaction a prospect has with you. Make sure they can find it. And when they do, make sure it is interesting, interactive and relevant so they will keep coming back. Be sure the visitor can add themselves to your database by signing up for your e-newsletter or downloading an e-paper.*

Web First

The first step should be an update of your web site to ensure that it is interactive, interesting and communicates the right messaging and positioning for your new business focus. Look at other marketing services providers' web sites to see what they have done, and this will give you good ideas as to the type of approach you should take. You can start with the five companies we profiled in Chapter Two of this book.

Why start with the web? Because all of your marketing efforts will include a push and pull to get recipients to visit your site.

Sure, you will need to have a presence on social media channels such as Facebook, Twitter, LinkedIn, YouTube, and more. But the majority of people will go to your web site to investigate your business.

Your web site needs to be in alignment with your strategy and portray the proper image. Even if you are using personalized URLs, there should be a way for folks to navigate to your main site from their personalized microsite. If the first thing they see when they get there is an image of some new piece of equipment or a lovely shot of your building, you will lose most of them. The content needs to be compelling and portray a customer focus. There must be something there for them to benefit from or they won't come back. People are too busy these days; they hate to waste their time. So you must make your web content relevant, and you must keep it fresh in order to keep them coming back.

NOTE: People will find your web site from a variety of channels, often by them taking action (searching, reading, etc). This is one facet of inbound marketing. Inbound marketing is a marketing strategy that focuses on getting found by customers. This is related to relationship marketing and Seth Godin's idea of permission marketing. David Meerman Scott recommends that marketers "earn their way in" (via publishing helpful information on a blog, etc.). This is in contrast to outbound marketing where you have to "buy, beg, or bug you way in" via paid advertisements, issuing press releases in the hope they get picked up by the trade press, or paying commissioned sales people, respectively.

Do you have a mobile web site? Yep, you need that too. In today's mobile world, more and more people will find you via their phones. It's not that hard. Visit iFlyMobi.com to learn more.

And remember, when you think about your web site, always keep in mind that in today's world, it is estimated that 70% of people look at a web site to do research before buying products or services from a company. What does your web site say about who you are and what you do?

Online Marketing (referred to as "Internet Marketing" in Wikipedia) is another term you will hear a great deal. Internet marketing refers to the placement of media at the many different stages of the customer engagement cycle through search engine marketing (SEM), search engine optimization (SEO), banner ads on specific web sites, e-mail marketing, and Web 2.0 strategies. In 2008, *The New York Times*—working with comScore—published an initial estimate to quantify the user data collected by large Internet-based companies. Counting four types of interactions with company web sites in addition to the hits from advertisements served from advertising networks, the authors found the potential for collecting data upward of 2,500 times on average per user per month.

Both inbound and online marketing need to be part of your marketing services provider tool chest.

Market Your Own Company

I have seen many successful marketing service providers that have begun the transformation from a commodity-based business. They have changed their web site, and they have stopped showing all of their equipment. That is a good first step, because marketing departments really don't care about your equipment. They care that you understand their business and their needs, and they like a web site that is crystal clear in representing what your business can do for them in terms of helping them meet their marketing goals and objectives. Sure, they may ask for an equipment list at some point, and you should have one available. But it is no longer the centerpiece of how you represent your business. Marketers want to know that you can help them execute in an innovative, yet cost-effective manner. They want to know that you understand their industry and their business. They especially like the ability to measure results, because they are increasingly being asked to measure their results against the dollars they are spending, and many of them simply do not have the tools and the time to get this done. This is the type of information that should be front and center on your company's web site.

> **TIP: *Customers are looking for a customer-focused experience. Today's communications are more about the customer and solving their business problems than they are about you and your products/services.***

So it is critical to get your web site in place first and to ensure that it reflects the proper branding and positioning. Your marketing plan should contain the direction that will enable your organization to execute this. Revisit the mini marketing plan contained in Chapter Four, the expanded marketing plan contained in Appendix B, and the resource materials available on the online resource page for this book to gain additional ideas about how you might implement this.

The goal is to make it very clear to web site visitors who you are and what you do. But the messaging needs to be developed with a customer focus in mind—that is, what are the questions the visitor is trying to answer for his or her business, and how can you help address them? Otherwise, you will continue to be identified in the minds of customers and prospects as a commodity mailer, or a fulfillment house, or even a printer, and may miss many potential opportunities to expand and grow your business.

Is Everyone On the Same Page?

A very important aspect of marketing your company is marketing it internally. That may sound a little silly. After all, people that work for you must know what the company is all about, right? Well, not necessarily. This is something you do not want to leave to chance. Every employee is a sales person for your company, and every employee should be able to concisely state your value proposition, your elevator pitch, your 118 seconds. This education can be done a number of ways, depending on the size of your organization. Perhaps you can have regular monthly Pizza Fridays[25] where you spend time bringing the staff up to date on the latest developments. If you are a

---

[25] You could have "free beer Fridays" as well. This might increase the excitement around the meeting, but everyone might forget what you have said by the end of it.

larger company, you may want to establish a formal training curriculum for all employees so that new employees come up to speed quickly and existing employees attend periodic refresher courses. Either way, your employees are important emissaries for your business, and keeping them on track with your branding, positioning and strategy helps them represent you better. It also improves employee satisfaction, since they feel more included.

Interactive Marketing Checklist

Use this checklist to see what you are (or are not) doing currently to market your business:

☐   Do you have a web site? Does it represent your business in the best possible light?

o   Is your web site interactive, interesting and frequently updated?

o   Who in your organization is responsible for keeping your web site current? How important is this task as compared to other duties? If it is not high on the list, it may not get done.

o   Do you have a blog? Blogs that are updated regularly encourage visitors to return, as well as to comment. Your goal should be to get as many customers as possible to subscribe to and participate in your blog.

o   Do you have any downloadable information? This is the information age, after all. If you have any tip sheets, white papers, case studies or other relevant information, you should provide this for your visitors…you can require them to sign in with an email address to get the download, thus enabling you to contact them later via email.

o   Do you have any audio or video on your web site? Not everyone likes to wade through pages of reading. Many would rather watch a quick video or listen to an audio recording. Just make sure your audio and video are web optimized so they download quickly. Video can also be replicated on your YouTube channel. (Do you have one?)

☐ Do you have any social networking profiles? Chapter Nine has a wealth of information about social media. At a minimum, you should have a presence on LinkedIn, Twitter and Facebook. A YouTube channel is an added bonus.

  o Who in your organization is responsible for your social media presence? Do they have time to dedicate to this important marketing aspect?

  o Are there guidelines in place to ensure appropriate content?

  o Do you personally have a social media presence? If not, you are making a mistake. Allocate the time to participate so that you gain a good understanding of what goes on in the social media sphere. How else will you be able to decide what types of social media services your business can sell?

☐ Do you reach your prospects through alternative means? Traditional marketing—direct mail, newspaper, TV, etc.— will likely still play an important role in your own self-promotion as well as the services you provide to customers. But you should also be using all or some of the following in your own self-promotional efforts. Walk the talk!

  o Email marketing

    ▪ Newsletters

    ▪ Auto responders

  o Personalized URLs and/or QR codes

  o Is the target audience mobile? Use a QR Code as an alternative response mechanism. The individual can scan the code and be driven to a mobile-friendly web page to respond to or interact with. Sometimes just a general URL can be used to drive people to a response form, but you should at least use a unique URL or identifier/shortener to track the response method.

  o Online ads/banners

Relevancy is Key

Today more than ever before, relevant communications are critical. If you send a communication to someone—whether it is printed or electronic—and it does not grab their interest, it will be deleted or tossed into the round file. No one has time to read everything that comes across their desks; you know that from personal experience.

There are six dimensions of marketing relevancy in the solutions that you will provide to clients and in your own marketing communications:

1. **Relevancy in Content**: providing the right information in the right context

2. **Relevancy in Contact**: delivering this information to the right people

3. **Relevancy in Channel**: providing it to the right medium in the right format

4. **Relevancy in Time**: delivering this information when it is appropriate to meet the recipient's needs

5. **Relevancy in Media:** providing the information in a format preferred by the recipient.

6. **Relevancy in Response Mechanism**: providing a way for people to respond that they can easily take advantage of, and that fits with their communications style.

Quick Plug: If you are in the mailing & fulfillment industries, and especially if you have added or are thinking of adding printing services, please make sure that you are familiar with InfoTrends. It is the leading worldwide market research and strategic consulting firm for the digital imaging and document solutions industry. InfoTrends provides research, analysis, forecasts, and advice to help clients understand market trends, identify opportunities, and develop strategies to grow their businesses. They have produced a lot of content to help service providers focus on relevancy. And they have done a great deal of research in the cross-media arena.

One more Quick Plug: You should also consider joining MFSA (Mailing & Fulfillment Service Association) if you have not already done so. This is your industry trade association, and your participation will bring value to you and your colleagues.

Your Self-Promotion Portfolio

The types of communications you should be considering for promotion of your own business mirror those you will sell to clients. They include:

1. **One-to-one ROI-driven multi-channel relationship marketing solutions** that are designed to deliver individual communications to the best and most profitable customers, create unique and customized messages across multiple channels, manage campaigns, track expenses, and calculate ROI in real time. To do this, you must have the right infrastructure in place. See Chapter Five for the detailed discussion.

2. **Data modeling and data mining** to determine the "sweet spot" based on specific criteria established by data experts. This is a service you can always outsource. Profiling factors such as demographics, product affinity, lifestyle, and cluster analysis enable the modeling of existing customer data against scrubbed national consumer files, extracting important and relevant demographics as well as lifestyle data. This means that you can model the trends and traits of your best customers and then use that "model" to find thousands more just like them. Hire a data expert or find a solid partner and try it first in your own self-promotional efforts. First-hand experience is the best way for you to learn how to sell what can appear to be a very complex service. It is complex—no question, but often painted to be more complex than it needs to be. With the right resources in place, it will add extreme value to the services you can offer.

3. **Web-based mailing, print and fulfillment solutions** for remote access to digital and physical assets for distributed sales representatives as well as agents and franchisees. These online storefronts are custom-designed for client organizations. They provide marketers, salespeople, and customers with 24-hour access to digital and physical assets. Users can customize the pieces and then download them immediately, or have prints delivered on demand. They can order personalized promotional materials, apparel, or other

approved non-printed items. Why not establish your own storefront for your sales and customer service representatives? How much time do they spend creating letters, presentations, emails and even flyers and brochures? How accurately do these materials reflect your corporate branding? Save time and standardize communications to protect your brand integrity while allowing your employees to customize materials in line with branding guidelines. If they use the service themselves, they can better explain its value to their customers.

4.   **A digital asset management system** must be in place to house all of the digital assets you and your clients will use in marketing efforts. This includes graphics, logos, templates, audio, video and more. A good digital asset management system ensures access to the most current version and includes security controls to prevent access by unauthorized users. Your digital asset management system should be able to handle digital assets, of course, but can also be used to track physical assets.

5.   **Comprehensive marketing program measurement metrics and analytics** are available through marketing dashboards. With a dashboard, you and/or your customers can:

- See who is responding within seconds of the visit
- Use up-to-date collected results for ROI calculations
- Create graphical representations of results that update automatically
- Improve sales lead effectiveness via automatically delivered lead e-mail messages
- Gain immediate access to raw data for other corporate systems or processes

6.   **Printing services** includes more than just putting ink and toner on paper and shipping it out the door. As a mailing/fulfillment service provider, you already have many of the pieces in place to add value to printing services. And printing presses are easier to use than ever before—digital, DI and even offset. You are already working with clients to minimize the impact of postage increases (or should be!) while maintaining response rates. Marketing services

providers consult with clients to discuss options such as modified packaging, address quality, bar-coding, delivery point verification, volume discounts, and other money-saving ideas. With printing services under your roof, it is one more arrow in your value-added quiver that will attract and keep loyal customers.

7. It goes without saying that **best-in-class mailing and fulfillment services** using the latest technology are table stakes in today's market. But by expanding your scope beyond mailing by equipping yourself to provide integrated marketing services to clients, you can solidify and increase their presence with existing customers and help them bring in new customers to grow their businesses. Obviously, the same applies to your self-promotional efforts.

First-Mover Advantage

Back in the "dot-com boom" days, the term "first-mover advantage"[26] came into quite heavy use. Each of those dot-com companies thought they had a better mousetrap and tons of money was poured into helping them be the first to market with a new idea—thus, the "first mover."

While many of those companies did not, in the end, succeed, those that did demonstrated the value being "first mover" can have. While more mailing & fulfillment operations are starting to make the move to transform their businesses, the industry has not reached critical mass, by a long shot. It is likely that within your own sphere of influence, you may be able to grab first-mover advantage. But you must move quickly to do so. Keep in mind that developing both the execution skills and the ability to articulate the advantages of your new services grows out of experimenting with your own business and your own self-promotion efforts.

In addition to the self-promotion examples contained in this book, you will find additional examples of specific campaigns that

---

[26] According to Wikipedia, "**First-mover advantage** is the advantage gained by the initial occupant of a market segment. This advantage may stem from the fact that the first entrant can gain control of resources that followers may not be able to match. Sometimes the first mover is not able to capitalize on its advantage, leaving the opportunity for another firm to gain **second-mover advantage**.

your peers have successfully deployed on the online resource page for this book, with metrics,.

Also, please visit http://www.NewPathToProfit.com for a list of associations that you may want to consider joining. There are many that provide valuable help and resources in the form of peer groups, case studies, webinars, conferences, and more.

Now What?

If you find yourself scratching your head after looking at the checklists above, wondering how to get started, all is not lost! That's why you're reading this book, and that's why you should be able to depend on the businesses and suppliers who support the industry to help guide you as you make the move to becoming a marketing services provider by learning how to efficiently market your own company using today's technology.

TIP: You are your first customer for marketing services.

Use the marketing campaign checklist below to create your first campaign. Keep in mind that once you have specific solutions in place, you will have access to much more specific guidance in regard to implementing those solutions from your supplier(s). But in the interim, this checklist will give you insight into how to get started on a specific campaign.

Guide to Creating a Successful Marketing Campaign

Name of Campaign/Event:

Date of Event:

Target Audience: Who is my target audience? Where will I source the data?

Key Message: What is the key message about your business that you are trying to convey?

Business Objective: What are you trying to achieve? How will you measure your success?

Offer: What offer are you extending to encourage recipients to respond?

Channels / Media:

- Print
- Direct Mailer
- Dimensional Mailer
- Electronic
- eMail
- Mobile/SMS
- Old Fashioned ;)
- Hand delivery

Creative: What will the design theme be? How will it be carried across multiple media to deliver an integrated campaign?

If the campaign starts with a postcard or other direct mailer, will you also send an email blast at some point?

- If so, at what point will it be sent? Will it be sent to the whole list, or only to the people that have or haven't responded?

If the campaign starts with email, will you also send a printed mailer or postcard at some point?

- If so, at what point will it be sent? Will it be sent to the whole list, only to the people that have or haven't responded and/or to email bounces?

Interactive (Landing Page) – will you require an access code to proceed? In many cases, a generic (not personalized) landing page, sometimes called a GURL (Generalized URL) can be effective, particularly if you do not have extensive information about recipients. This is a way to get interested parties engaged in a dialog and begin to collect more individual information that can make future communications more personalized and relevant. A GURL should contain:

- Response Page (confirm or collect contact details)
- Survey Page (ask two to three questions to get the dialog going; the campaign offer should be compelling enough to encourage recipients to spend the time and give up the information)
- Offer page (this is where the respondents can take advantage of your offer)
- Thank-You Page. Be sure to thank recipients for participating!

Personalized URLs and/or QR Codes. Will you be using personalized URLs and/or QR Codes to drive people to personalized landing pages? If so, which domain will you use? See the Personalized URL Checklist below.

Email Response
Will a Thank You email automatically be sent to people that respond?

Due Dates

- Creative approval –
- File sent to Printer -
- Landing Page –
- Mailing –
- Responses –

Personalized URL Checklist

If you are including personalized URLs in your campaign, use this checklist to make sure you don't miss anything.

This process may vary depending upon the application you are using to create and manage personalized URLs. While this process describes the creation of an email campaign with personalized URLs, a similar process can also be used to create printed pieces. Check with your software provider for details.

1. Set up your client's reporting dashboard to specifically apply to their campaigns.

2. Purchase a URL for personalized URLs through a site such as NetworkSolutions.com or GoDaddy.com. Point the URL to the DNS address of application servers for your

personalized URL solution (this information is supplied by your software provider).

3. Build the mailing list (this may be supplied to you by the customer, you may need to purchase it, or if you've done a campaign recently for them, it might be a list of people that did not respond to a previous mailer).

4. Determine if recipients of the mailers will need to enter an Access Code when they go to their personalized URL.

5. Upload the mailing list to your marketing software.

6. Generate personalized URLs for those contacts (and Access Codes, if necessary).

7. Check for any duplicate personalized URLs, and modify accordingly.

8. Export the mailing list along with the personalized URLs (and Access Codes, if necessary).

9. Work with your customer to identify which areas of the landing page will be personalized.

10. Review the artwork on the direct mail piece (or email). What creative elements should be re-used on the landing page?

11. Identify a proposed layout for the landing page (perhaps using templates that are provided by your software provider).

12. Build the landing page, incorporating creative elements from the original media.

13. Add questions or a survey to the landing page to help gather additional information on each recipient.

14. Set up contact fields on the landing page so that recipients can verify or update their contact information.

15. Ensure that if someone accesses an invalid personalized URL or simply types in the General URL, that they either are rejected or they can view the page as a guest (in that scenario, they will be added to the system as a new contact).

16. Set up the personalization rules on the landing page.

17. Create a Thank You page that people will see after they submit their landing page response.

18. If any of the questions should have resulted in providing electronic fulfillment or hardcopy fulfillment, set this up through your software solution.

19. Put a Redirect URL or other links on the Thank You page, to help continue the dialog. This can be directed to the customer's home page, or a specific page on their web site that is relevant to the campaign.

20. Set up an Auto-Response Email that can be instantly sent to people that submit the form (optional).

21. Ensure that the proper sales reps are set up to be notified when people visit their landing page.

22. Create personalized URLs for your Seed list.

23. TEST, TEST, TEST!

With the right software solution in place, you can also:

- Notify the application of the URL and landing page relationship
- Create new keywords for campaigns
- Track emails/bounces

On to Selling!

Now that you have given some thought to how you will promote your new services, we'll now move on to the sales process—how it differs from what you might be doing today, and how you can change the types of relationships you have with customers. This is the topic of Chapter Eight.

Keys to Success

- Traditional marketing still works!! Marketing fundamentals are just that – fundamentals. They don't change a whole lot. Technology, however, has opened up a whole new world for you to use when you market.

- Your first step should be an update of your web site to ensure that it is interactive, interesting and communicates the right messaging and positioning for your new business focus.

- Marketers want to know that you can help them execute in an innovative, yet cost-effective manner. They are not that interested in your equipment list.

- A very important aspect of marketing your company is marketing it internally. Your staff must be able to clearly articulate your value proposition.

- Today more than ever before, relevant communications are critical.

- The types of communications you should be considering for promotion of your own business mirror those you will sell to clients.

- Developing both the execution skills and the ability to articulate the advantages of your new services grows out of experimenting with your own business and your own self-promotion efforts.

- You are your first customer. Use the marketing campaign checklist included in this chapter to create your first campaign.

CHAPTER EIGHT

YOUR GUIDE TO SELLING MARKETING SERVICES

Increase Your Customer's Profit First, and Good Things Happen to You

This chapter is not meant to be a tutorial on selling; there are plenty of other resources out there that meet that need. Rather, it is designed to point out some of the differences in the sales process that are required as you transform your business from a mailing & fulfillment business to a marketing services provider. This chapter is primarily focused on what is known as "solution selling," and there are also many books available on that topic for your edification and further education. Just search the term on Amazon. A recent search turned up 54 different options if you want to dive deeper into that subject.

Let me begin with an example to frame the discussion. In a classic marketing services provider use case, I like to cite the example of how a marketing services provider approaches a marketing department to sell an entire seminar. This demonstrates the end-to-end solution sales approach and customer focus that is required to be successful in this new business. My good friend Joe Truncale, President of NAPL[27], once said, "I can hardly wait for the day when a sales rep who printed and distributed all of the materials for one of our events actually comes back to me and asks how the session went—is there follow-up needed? Is there anything we could have done better? How can we help your next event be better? After all, he has all of the information about the event because he produced and distributed the materials. It still hasn't happened yet!"

As Truncale indicates, a seminar requires planning for its promotion, production, follow-up and the next seminar next quarter or next year. This includes registering attendees, mail and email notifications of various types, collection of registration fees (the e-commerce component), thank you cards, seminar information in printed and electronic form, directions, and booklets and on-site materials to be organized and printed, as well as surveys to be taken and followed up on. That is a big effort for any marketing department, with a lot of moving pieces. It is also an area where marketing services providers can offer invaluable assistance. Marketing departments are strapped for resources. They don't have enough people. It is a classic example of a product a marketing services provider can sell—and perhaps even specialize in.

But there are a lot of moving pieces, most of which are time critical, must be accomplished accurately and may require coordination of external resources. As with our discussion about self-

---

[27] National Association for Printing Leadership (www.NAPL.org)

promotion, a good way to get your feet wet selling this solution—and in the process learn how to sell solutions—is to try conducting your own event. Document everything, and at its conclusion, you will have a handy handbook that you can use in selling your services to customers and demonstrating your knowledge and expertise in this arena.

> *TIP: Selling a set of packaged services designed to help customers conduct more effective seminars can be a good start in the marketing services business.*

Driving the Sales Process with Marketing Automation

But let's back up for a moment. Before you start selling anything, you need to have an effective sales organization in place. You should also have a formalized sales process in place that guides your sales professionals through a series of repeatable steps. This has multiple advantages:

- It standardizes your sales process;

- It makes it easier for sales managers to do their job;

- Over time you can actually begin to better predict a sales cycle for more accurate forecasting; and

- It can be modified and refined over time as you learn from your sales activities, ultimately creating a sure-fire sales process that works for you and your team.

- Having a formal sales process in place also makes it easier to hire and train new sales personnel.

This sales process should never, ever start with a cold call. Delivering qualified leads to your sales force is an important outcome of your marketing efforts. Cold calling has the lowest return on investment of all prospecting methods. Think about the cost of having a sales person "dialing for dollars" all day, or worse, driving around her territory, knocking on doors that don't want to open. In addition, sales people typically do not like cold calling. If you insist on cold calling, it can often lead to sales turnover, which costs you dearly.

Sales calls are expensive. To the extent you can leverage your marketing efforts to raise awareness and make those sales calls more effective, you will be doing your company a tremendous service. Let's look at a simplistic example.

- Assume your sales rep costs you $125,000 per year for salary, commissions, field expenses and benefits
- There are approximately 223 work days in a year
- Assume your sales rep is making an average of four sales calls per day for an annual total of 892 sales calls.
- You have an average close rate of 35%.

Now let's do the math.

$$\$125,000 / 892 = \$140 \text{ per sales call}$$

In this scenario, every sales call costs you $140. More likely, the actual number is much higher once travel expenses and other costs are factored in. And with a 35% close rate, that means that 580 of those sales calls never turn into orders, costing you about $80,000. Or put another way, you are spending $125,000 for 312 successful sales calls, or $400 per successful sales call.

Of course, not every qualified lead will turn into a sale. We all know that. But with an effective sales process in place, and marketing efforts to deliver qualified leads, you may be surprised at the difference you will see in sales productivity. The key to the sales process is to make it measurable. That's where sales and marketing automation come in to play.

Sales Force Automation (SFA)

Sales force automation, or a sales force management system, is generally part of a customer relationship management (CRM) system, especially when sales force automation is linked to marketing automation (more on that below). Sales force automation records all of the stages in a sales process. It also includes a contact management system that tracks all contacts with individual customers.

Other capabilities of a sales force automation system include:

- Sales lead tracking system

- Sales forecasting
- Order management
- Product knowledge

Anyone in your company who has customer contact should have access to the sales automation system. That prevents duplication of efforts and also ensures that anyone having contact with the customer has the latest update on that customer's status, and in turn, can update status after his actions are complete.

The sales force automation system not only makes sales reps more productive, but it makes their management more streamlined. Sales managers can keep their fingers on the pulse of sales activities, spending time where it is most advantageous in selling and training activities. It also ensures that performance appraisals are fact-based, taking much of the emotion and subjectivity out of the process.

Of course, for a system of this nature to be effective, sales personnel must be thorough in keeping it updated, and managers must be relentless in making sure this happens. A sales automation system that is either portable—and can be synchronized with the master system when the sales rep is in the office—or web-based, allowing real-time updates from anywhere with an Internet connection, make keeping the system updated much less of a chore. Reps can quickly add information at the conclusion of a sales call from a computer or smart phone, ensuring more accurate input and increased completeness of each customer record.

TIP: Your sales force automation system should be the centerpiece of your new sales process. It should have a mobile-friendly component

---

The sales force automation system is obviously beneficial to sales professionals and their managers. But it is also of great benefit to the marketing department. As your customer database builds, your marketing department can use the system to do a number of things, including:

- Finding out who your most profitable customers are. This is a good first step in profiling your target markets. A marketer can "clone" those most profitable customers by seeking other customers just like them, targeting marketing efforts to develop more qualified leads.

- Better understanding the competition. If a sales rep loses a deal, that should be documented in the system, including who the competitor was. A marketer can analyze trends across sales reps and help develop a stronger competitive strategy.

- Coordinating the sales function with other parts of the marketing mix. For example, if you are conducting a self-promotional campaign, that information should be entered into the sales force automation system, including who was contacted, what their responses were and more.

- Analysis of sales activities can also help you refine your sales process, yielding clear trends that demonstrate what works and what doesn't based on the actual closing of deals.

A variety of sales force automation systems are available in the marketplace, including ACT! from Sage; Goldmine from FrontRange Solutions; SalesForce.com; SugarCRM; and (plug alert!) interlinkONE..

Also, you can visit http://www.NewPathToProfit.com to access a competitive matrix that interlinkONE has published comparing various vendors in this space.

Marketing Automation

The term "marketing automation" is a mouthful – but it's one that is worth understanding. Using technology to build a marketing campaign and send out consistent, relevant messages in an efficient, cohesive manner is always a good thing! So if you're a little tech-hesitant, don't get scared off by the term. Marketing automation is really all about making your marketing easier on you and more effective overall. A marketing automation solution enables you to automate marketing functions, including campaign creation, market segmentation and response analysis.

There are several things that are important when it comes to marketing automation. As you read through these benefits, you should also be thinking about how to integrate marketing and sales automation efforts.

1. Marketing automation simplifies the gathering of data that can be used to target your audience in a relevant and valued way. Think about all the information that could be collected

about your target market. And think about how much could be collected over a period of time to establish history and forward-looking trends. That kind of information is worth its weight in gold, don't you think? To be able to see the habits of your audience, pre-determine their likely decisions based on historical data…it's a gold mine at your fingertips. Marketing automation software enables this data collection and analysis, and it's obvious how important this information is for your future marketing campaigns. Why shoot in the dark for leads when you don't have to?

2. Marketing automation delivers the ability to build a multi-channel campaign that reaches your target market(s) within the channel(s) they prefer using their preferred media. Your audience resides in a vast universe. And not all of the residents of that universe will respond to a message sent via a single channel. Imagine resting your marketing campaign on a banner ad. Okay, so the banner ad is placed on several highly visible sites that your audience frequents. And the banner ad is actually pretty cool, and you received great feedback when you tested it. But not everyone clicks on banner ads. Many people may turn a blind eye to them after cruising the Internet for too long. Multi-channel campaigns allow you to send a consistent marketing message across several channels. Email. Direct mail. Text messages. Even strategically positioned signs and displays. Larger campaigns that seemed unmanageable with your current manpower are within your grasp when you implement a marketing automation solution.

3. Marketing automation lets you develop an information map for your audience. You can make it easy for your prospects to find the information they need by having a clear call to action and the ability to follow through when they do contact you or respond to your activities. Landing pages, personalized URLs…when your call to action is combined with an offer, your prospects are incented to move, heading to the automated responses that you have set into place. And in fact, as they move forward and receive those automatic responses, your sales team is in the wings, waiting to work the warm and hot leads.

4. The ability to score your leads. Not every lead is created equal. This goes back to the need to ferret out the most qualified leads to feed to your expensive sales force. Some people are ready to buy. Some need more time and information. Some are just looky-loos that are browsing with no real intention to buy anything. You don't have the time or resources to waste on the leads that aren't ready. So one of the best things about an automated marketing solution is its lead scoring capability, quickly informing your sales team who is cold and who is hot!

5. Marketing automation also allows you to associate inventory with the survey that you have set up on your lead capture forms. Based on how a person responds, you may be able to set up an automated follow-up that provides links to electronic materials that may appeal to that person, based on the answers they selected. Or it may generate a hardcopy fulfillment order that is mailed to the respondent, based on how they requested their follow-up information.

6. At the heart of any marketing automation solution is the ability to measure the results of campaigns. If you throw a marketing campaign out there, you want to know what parts of it were a hit and what parts were a miss. Did the email message fall flat? Was the text message the best received? Did you hit a home run with the QR Codes? The more you can analyze, the better, because it will enable you to design and implement further campaigns that are even more successful.

Scan this QR Code for more information on Marketing Automation

Marketing Automation and the Sales Funnel

Everything starts with the top – the largest ring – the target market. And then it narrows down from there as the true qualified leads are generated. As those leads are worked, some remain as the funnel narrows, turning into sales. But where does marketing automation fit into the sales funnel? At what point does the automated system kick in and help make that sales funnel work?

At the top of the funnel is the target market. This is the group of people you know your products or services can benefit. You create your campaign, choosing the various channels (email, social media, direct mail, mobile, etc.) you wish to use to reach your market, ensuring that the messages remain consistent across all channels. Each of these messages includes a call to action. As you begin to get responses from that larger group, your campaign can respond with further communications using personalized landing pages and direct mail.

With an automated marketing solution, your efforts across all channels are tracked in real time and data are compiled. These data are useful for analyzing the current campaign as well as refining and streamlining future campaign efforts. But more importantly, the automated marketing solution allows for personalized responses to go back out to these new leads, warming them up for the sales team.

What warms up the leads even more is nurturing them through a multi-touch response campaign. Depending upon the response mechanism used by the prospect, the next automated contact will be initiated. Did they respond via email or through a general web page? Perhaps the next contact will be an e-newsletter or a personalized email with a personalized URL. Or you could choose to send a direct mailer or postcard to highly qualified respondents. Each of these events is automated, and each lead receives multiple contacts.

TIP: Multiple touches are the rule of the day. Don't depend on one channel or one contact to make your point or that of your customer. Get a dialog going. Today's communications should be two-way!

Throughout these contacts, all data are still being tracked and compiled. The sales team is kept in the loop and even assigned tasks that fall in line with the automated system. Perhaps a prospect has clicked on a personalized URL and indicated an interest in receiving more information. They may even have asked for a sales representative to contact them. The sales team will know about each contact and what the lead is looking for so when that phone call is made, all of the ground work has already been laid.

Figure 19. Sample Funnel Metrics

Once a sale is concluded, the customer service department can move in to help ensure a terrific customer experience. At that point, the marketing automation solution can be used to perform an analysis, generating performance metrics that make it clear what worked and what didn't. From the top of the sales funnel to the bottom, marketing automation helps to ensure that a marketing campaign is consistent, efficient and capable of being analyzed for the benefit of future campaigns.

The Role of Marketing as a Lead Generator

Sales people should only be selling to the prospects that the marketing department leads to their doorstep. Think about it…if the marketing department falls short and fails to deliver the marketing message to the target market, then the whole sales process crumbles.

Figure 20. Sample Funnel Metrics: Another View

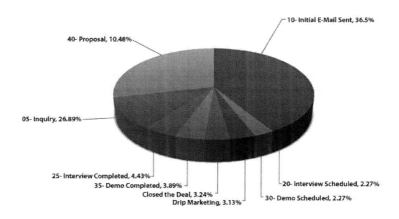

It is the job of the marketing department to find the prospects and lure them in. The sales department seals the deal. With marketing automation, a sales department can rest assured that a campaign is working like clockwork to bring the target market to the doorstep. For sales, lead generation is essential.

In addition, with marketing automation, everything is tracked and managed from one central spot. Instead of the right hand (sales) not knowing what the left hand (marketing) is doing, the two hands are working in conjunction, as a team. With an automated marketing system, tasks and contacts are managed, and prospects can be touched multiple times without feeling overwhelmed and turned off by a pushy company.

Let's look at a specific example of how an automated campaign might be constructed. Let's say your sales team exhibits at a local business expo. Several people fill out the lead form requesting more information about your products or services. That is the beginning of the lead generation process, participation in an event that was set up by the marketing department. Here is what happens afterwards.

marketing functions, including campaign creation, market segmentation and response analysis.

- Marketing automation simplifies the gathering of data that can be used to target your audience in a relevant and valued way.

- Marketing automation delivers the ability to build a multi-channel campaign that reaches your target market(s) within the channel(s) they prefer using their preferred media. Your audience resides in a vast universe.

- One of the best things about an automated marketing solution is the lead scoring capability, quickly informing your sales team who is cold and who is hot!

- At the heart of any marketing automation solution is the ability to measure the results of campaigns.

- With an automated marketing solution, your efforts across all channels are tracked in real time and data are compiled.

- It is the job of the marketing department to find the prospects and lure them in. The sales department seals the deal.

CHAPTER NINE

SOCIAL MEDIA: WHAT IS IT AND WHERE DOES IT FIT?

Why Engaging with Customers and Prospects on Social Media is Good for Business

Figure 21. Content Distribution Strategy

Distribution Strategy

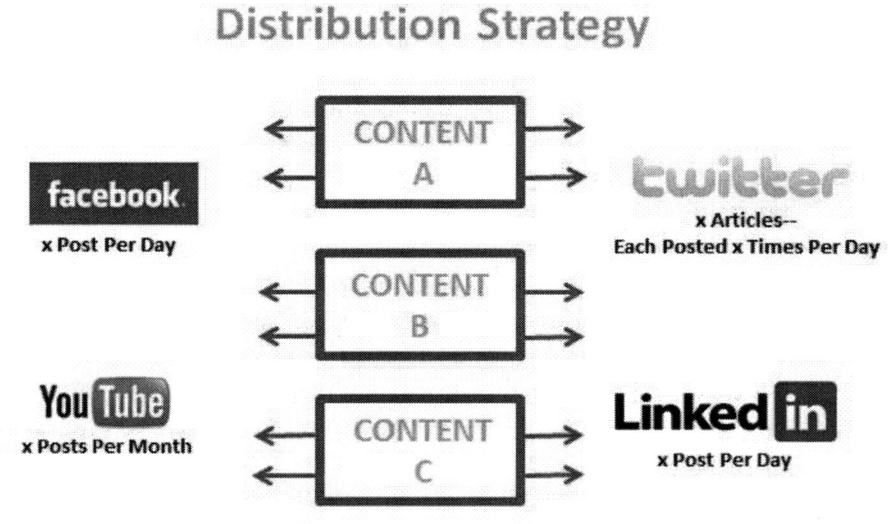

Figure 21 helps demonstrate how you should view your social media channels in relation to your website – the promotion should work both ways.

How can you use social media for your marketing services provider business?

- Brand promotion

- Building buzz

- Customer / prospect interaction

- Tracking your online reputation

Why is branding important in social media? My answer is: "It is your brand! Protect it and use it!" From the name you acquire as your Twitter username right down to the graphics you use on your social media pages, you must view these types of decisions as important and as items that can enhance or detract from your brand.

But there are so many social media sites out there that it can be confusing. Which sites should you build your profile on? On how many sites should you create a presence? And how are you going to keep up with it all?

The number one tip I can offer is to have an online marketing plan. Your plan will incorporate your strategy for deploying and measuring the tactics you will use online.

Top Social Media Sites for Marketing Services Providers

The danger of creating profiles on more than a handful of social media sites is that you spread yourself too thin. You end up failing to create any buzz or relating to any prospects on any of the sites. So it is important to choose a small number of sites where you can easily maintain a presence.

One thing to keep in mind is that everything you do on these social media sites is online and public. So keeping everything on a professional level is critical. You don't want to do anything to damage your business reputation. That is why companies like Coca-Cola invest significant efforts in monitoring sites like Facebook and removing objectionable content that doesn't comply with its House Rules. That doesn't mean removing anything the company doesn't like. For example, in the debate about whether Coca-Cola should be using sugar instead of high fructose corn syrup, one user posted an opinion that Pepsi was better. That was not removed, nor should it have been. In social media, you do not want to censor, but as your communities grow, you may find it beneficial to publish rules as Coke did, and then manage the site according to those rules.

TIP: Monitoring social media is not about censorship.

So…where should you concentrate your social media efforts? There are three top social media sites that are most likely to benefit your marketing services provider business—Twitter, Facebook and LinkedIn. First, let's describe what they are, and then I will provide a complete guide for using each of these sites. As you get more familiar with the social media universe, and as new sites start gaining traction, you may choose to add others to the mix. But these three are a good place to start.

Twitter: Wikipedia describes Twitter, created in 2006, as a free social networking and microblogging service that enables its users to send and read messages known as *tweets*. Tweets are text-based posts of up to 140 characters (including spaces) displayed on the author's profile page and delivered to the author's subscribers who are known as *followers*. Senders can restrict delivery to those in their circle of friends or, by default, allow open access. Ever since late 2009, users can follow lists of authors instead of following individual authors. All users can send and receive tweets via the Twitter website, Short Message Service (SMS) or external applications. While the service itself costs nothing to use, accessing it through SMS may incur phone service provider fees.

Although historically Twitter closely guarded its usage statistics, the company has become more open about volumes. In October of 2011, a Twitter blog post reported that Twitter users were sending 250 million tweets per day, compared to 2 million per day in January of 2009 and 65 million per day in mid-2010.

Even so, Twitter remains just a fraction of the size of Facebook (discussed next), who counts more than 800 million active users, more than half of which they claim log in at least once daily.

Tweets can be promotional in nature, informational, fun or entertaining—and should include a mix of these. Simply using it as a promotional tool will not be well-accepted by your community and could cause people to "unfollow" you as well as recommend the same to their friends. Ideally, your tweets should be "re-tweetable." This means that other Twitter users find it worthy of repeating your tweet to their group of followers. In this way, good content can actually go viral as it spreads from network to network. While Twitter may appear to be a one way conversation, it is anything but. You should be conversing and building relationships with others using this medium.

Facebook: According to Wikipedia,[28] Facebook, founded in February of 2004 from a Harvard University dorm room, is a social networking website that is operated and privately owned by Facebook, Inc. Users can add friends, send them messages, and update their

---

[28] Information and statistics about various social media venues cited in this document come from Wikipedia and other online sources (including published company data) as of February 2010

personal profiles to notify friends about themselves. Additionally, users can join networks organized by city, workplace, and school or college. The website's name stems from the colloquial name of books given at the start of the academic year by university administrations with the intention of helping students to get to know each other better. While Facebook may have started as a college/university phenomenon, the majority of Facebook users today are outside of colleges and universities.

Although these facts and figures change daily, they are worth reviewing. Simply search "Facebook Facts and Statistics" on Google to get current data.

- More than 800 million active users in 2011 (this grew from 150 million in January of 2009)

- More than 350 million active users currently accessing Facebook through their mobile devices

- 50% of active users log on to Facebook in any given day

- People spend over 700 billion minutes per month on Facebook and more than 30 billion pieces of content (web links, news stories, blog posts, notes, photo albums, etc.) are shared each month

- Average user is connected to 80 community pages, groups and events

- More than 2.5 million web sites have integrated with Facebook, including over 80 of comScore's U.S. Top 100 web sites and over half of comScore's Global Top 100 web sites..

- More than 700,000 local businesses have active Pages on Facebook

About 70% of Facebook users are outside of the United States.

Many companies have established business pages, such as Coca-Cola. Companies also often have evangelists who have their own Facebook and Twitter accounts, build their own online identities, gain their own followers, and can help promote online visibility of the company.

LinkedIn: LinkedIn is an interconnected network of professionals that has more than 101 million members in over 200 countries and territories around the world, with about half of the members being outside the U.S. The company claims that a new member joins LinkedIn approximately every second and more than one million companies have LinkedIn company pages. It is worth noting that according to LinkedIn, executives from all Fortune 500 companies are LinkedIn members.

LinkedIn allows registered users to maintain a list of contact details of people they know and trust in business. This builds up a contact network, and allows users to see connections of their connections (called second-degree connections). This can be utilized to gain introductions through a mutual, trusted friend. Users can also recommend other users, and these recommendations can be leveraged for various purposes. Users can find, be introduced to and collaborate with qualified professionals they need to work with to accomplish their goals.

LinkedIn also allows users to research companies that they may be interested in working with. When typing the name of a given company in the search box, statistics about the company are provided, as well as employees of that company registered with LinkedIn and their relationship (if any) to your network.

According to QuantCast, LinkedIn is visited by nearly 50 million people monthly worldwide (21 million U.S.).

At first glance, LinkedIn may appear to be a site that is useful for a job search or a way to rub shoulders with fellow colleagues. But it has evolved into so much more. You can update your profile page with your RSS feed, be "introduced" to new connections, join groups and ask questions. The atmosphere is definitely more professional in nature than Facebook, and it's the perfect addition to your social media efforts. A good way to get started with LinkedIn is to join groups and participate - demonstrate your company's and your own attributes. Engage in the group, show yourself as a thought leader.

In addition to these sites, you should consider establishing a blog. You can also begin to dip your toe into location-based marketing, one of the hottest social media growth areas. And don't forget video—not only should you consider placing brief video clips on your website—perhaps as a tutorial relevant to your business and your customers' needs, or as an explanation of a unique service you offer—but you can also easily produce and post videos on your own YouTube channel. Read on.

Foursquare

Foursquare is one of an emerging class of location-based services. It is a mobile application that makes cities easier and more interesting to explore. It is a friend-finder, a city social guide and a game that challenges users to experience new things while rewarding them for doing so. Foursquare lets users "check in" to a place when they're there, tell friends where they are and track the history of where they've been and who they've been there with.

As of June 2011, Foursquare was reporting over 10 million users worldwide, with more than 3 million check-ins per day. There are more than 400,000 businesses using the site's Merchant Platform, a free set of tools that helps businesses attract new customers and keep the best ones coming back. Registered users can connect with friends and update their location. Points are awarded for checking in at venues. Users can also earn badges by checking in at locations with certain tags, for check-in frequency or for other patterns, such as time of check-in. Users that check in the most times to a location, with a limit of one check-in per day, over a 60-day period are awarded the "mayorship" of the location until someone else succeeds them by checking in more times.

One example of how Foursquare is being used in a business sense was CNN's partnership with the site to promote a week-long series on healthy eating. During the promotion, "If you friend CNN on Foursquare and check in at one of 10,651 farmers markets across the globe, you'll get a 'Healthy Eater' badge." Dennis Crowley, the CEO of Foursquare, said, "We've seen time and time again how Foursquare can be used to drive people to action, and CNN's campaign is a perfect example of how brands can use the platform to promote good behavior, such as healthy eating."

As growth in mobile use continues with devices such as the Apple iPhone and iPad, Android phones and other GPS-enabled devices, marketers will increasingly look to location-based marketing for improved results. By experimenting with sites like Foursquare and other location-based social media venues, like Yelp, you will gain insight into the possibilities these emerging services present.

YouTube

YouTube is a video-sharing web site, currently owned by Google. Users can upload videos to share, and companies can establish "YouTube Channels." Founded in May of 2005, YouTube has partnership deals with content providers including major TV networks, music companies, etc. YouTube videos often "go viral," meaning people watch them, find them interesting, educational or amusing, and forward the link to friends. Many printers may remember the video posted by Warren Werbitt of Pazazz Printing entitled "Printing's Alive." As of this writing, it has had more than 236,000 views since it was posted three years ago. Pazazz Printing has six videos posted, including a TNT news report about its green initiatives and a new version of "Printing's Alive."

We call this humanizing your brand. Today, people are less inclined to do business with a company simply because of their logo or because they recognize the brand. Before they open their wallet, they want to know who is behind the curtain. Online video sites such as YouTube allow businesses to introduce their employees, passions, and interests to prospects and customers.

48 hours of video are uploaded every minute. More video is uploaded to YouTube in 60 days than the 3 major U.S. networks created in 60 years! It can be a powerful marketing platform if used correctly.

Google+

Google+ is a social network that was launched in the 2nd-half of 2011 to much fan-fare. As of this writing, more than 62 million users have signed up to use the service. While it contains similar features to Facebook and Twitter, simply having Google's backing makes it a social network worth paying attention to. (It seems that they have learned some valuable lessons from previous failures, including their Wave product!).

Blogs

Blog is a contraction of the term web log. A blog is a web site that is generally maintained by an individual with regular entries of commentary, descriptions of events or other material such as graphics or videos. There are also corporate blogs in addition to personal blogs, and most news outlets these days also have blogs, often with entries written by their leading columnists or commentators. *WhatTheyThink*, a leading online media outlet for the printing and publishing industries, has six different special-interest blogs, as an example, including The Web and Print, Economics & Research and Going Green.

Blogs are an excellent means of getting a discussion going. While it requires an authorized author to start a discussion track, anyone can post comments to a blog entry, and in the "blogosphere," or universe of blog readers and users, people typically are not shy about sharing their opinions on whatever topic is being discussed. Blogs can be moderated, meaning that an administrator reviews all comments before they go live. This allows you to prevent objectionable material from being posted to your blog. Be careful, however, in your censorship efforts, as we have advised before.

Technorati has issued an annual State of the Blogosphere study each year since 2004. In its 2010 report (its most recent as of this writing), the company indicates that there are more than 150 million web sites identified as blogs. A minority of bloggers are making money from their blogs, either by hosting advertising on their sites or by using their blogs to drive speaking engagements and traditional media assignments. Fourteen percent of those who have monetized their blogging are corporates. Universal McCann reports that 77% of Internet users read blogs.

TIP: Don't wait—jump in and start using these tools! Participate, engage and measure!

Twitter Basics for Marketing Services Providers

If you haven't already checked out Twitter and created a profile, what are you waiting for? Twitter is an excellent micro-blogging platform for spreading the word about company news, special events, discounts and more. Want to connect with prospects? Want to display your expertise? In 140 characters or less you can "tweet" tips, coupon codes, links to press releases…the sky is the limit. Here are some tips on how you can set your marketing services provider business up for success on Twitter.

Setting up your profile

Make sure you complete your profile. It needs to represent your company and further your brand, so upload your logo to use as your avatar[29]. Choose a Twitter name that is either your actual company name, or an easy-to-understand shorter version of your company name. Your one-line bio allows for 160 characters only, so try to use keywords that make your profile searchable, rather than a vague tagline or slogan. You may want to create a custom background for your Twitter page that utilizes your logo in some way and have it clearly show the web address of your company web site. If you choose to have individuals act as evangelists for you on Twitter, they should use their own photos as their avatars.

Finding people to follow

After you set up your Twitter profile, you want to "follow" other Twitter users. This allows you to see their tweets from your Twitter home page. As you follow others, you will find that many follow you back. You want to build up your list of followers, because these are people who will be able to regularly see your tweets as you make them.

Finding people to follow isn't difficult. Some of your customers may actually invite you to follow them, by placing a Twitter badge on their website or adding their Twitter profile URL to their email signature. You can also click on the "Find People" link at the top of the Twitter page. From there, you have several options: find people on Twitter via their name, business name, brand, keyword or Twitter handle (user name); find people via other networks such as Google, Yahoo! or AOL; invite people via email; or look at suggested users.

> **TIP:** *If someone follows you on Twitter, take the time to check them out and decide whether to follow them back.*

---

[29] An avatar is a computer user's representation of himself/herself or alter ego whether in the form of a three-dimensional model used in computer games, a two-dimensional icon (picture) or a one-dimensional username used on Internet forums and other communities. Source: Wikipedia, September 2010.

After you begin following people and businesses you already know, you can:

- Check out the followers of those Twitter users you admire. If you are following someone or a company and you like their tweets and admire the way they handle themselves online, then it makes sense to see who they are following and do so as well.

- Use the "find people" search option and search with keywords that your target market would use in their Twitter handles and profiles.

Tweet responsibly and responsively

You'll need to be creative at times to get your message down to 140 characters or less. In fact, your goal should be to make your tweet shorter so that others can "re-tweet" your message without editing…getting it more exposure. It's okay to toot your own horn, but try to make sure your Twitter stream isn't a constant barrage of sales pitches. And make sure to keep an eye on your messages. You may receive private messages via the "Direct Message" system, or you may receive a public tweet when someone includes your Twitter handle in a tweet. You should respond in kind when appropriate – no one likes a tweeter who only tweets about their own stuff. So keep in mind that Twitter is a conversational tool, not a one-way onslaught of your promotional tweets.

What to tweet about

There's plenty to tweet about. Here are some ideas:

- Links to your blog posts
- Links to your video or audio offerings
- Links to other online information (stats, blog posts, news articles/stories, videos, etc.) that you feel are relevant and useful to your followers
- Company announcements – from employee of the month to hitting your latest sales goal
- What you are currently working on
- What you are currently reading

- Events you are attending or organizing
- Retweet other tweets to cultivate relationships and help disseminate useful information
- Answers to questions that relate to your business, products/services
- Ask questions and invite commentary

Facebook Basics for Marketing Services Providers

Are you Facebooking your prospects and customers? With today's technology and the multiple ways you can interact with your prospects and get your message across, it's important to take advantage of the more popular social media sites where your prospects and customers hang out. Did you know that Facebook has over 500 million users? Don't you think your current and future customers are among them? So stop putting off the inevitable, and set up a Facebook business page so you can connect with prospects and customers, promote your products/services, and make the most of the content you put out (articles, videos, audios, etc.) about your products and services.

Keep in mind that there is a difference between personal and business accounts on Facebook. Business accounts are limited in the information they are able to access compared to standard accounts. You can't send or receive friend requests, for example. However, this shouldn't prevent you from creating a business page for your company. In fact, there are benefits to business pages, where you can designate multiple administrators to manage and post to the account. Also, the pages are public and therefore will attain rank in Facebook and search engine results. A business page can garner "fans" and you can post events, pictures, videos, polls and other interactive ways to promote your business and build the buzz.

TIP: Remember: profiles are personal but pages are business in Facebook world. You'll want to set up a page (not a profile). And remember to only create one account, because Facebook

> *doesn't take kindly to those who create multiple accounts.*

After you create your Facebook business page, you want people to "Like" your site.[30] Here are some ways you can build that base:

- Make sure your page is searchable by the general public. This is typically the default setting, but you may want to double-check by looking at Settings on the Edit page. Make sure your page is "Published" (publicly visible).

- Announce your new Facebook page on your web site / blog with a link to your page and an invitation to "Like" your page.

- If you have a newsletter, be sure to include the news about your new Facebook page.

- Send out an email to all your existing contacts asking them to check out your Facebook page, "Like" it and leave a post.

- Leverage your other social media profiles and invite those connections and followers to check you out on Facebook. For example, if you're active on Twitter, you should tweet the link to your Facebook page and ask your followers to "Like" your page.

- Post a Facebook badge or widget on your website to let your site visitors know about your Facebook page.

- Think about using Facebook ads. Yes, it costs some money, but the advertising will get your business name in front of a lot of eyeballs.

Of course, it will be easier to get more "fans" as you build your page and add content that is informative and engaging. Add polls, events, links and videos. Invite commentary by posting questions. Pull in the RSS feed from your blog. Post about special discounts or coupons. As you build on your page, current "fans" will share the page with their colleagues and friends and your base will grow.

Remember, Facebook is not just about information or entertainment. It's also about relationship building. Connect with your

---

[30] In 2010, Facebook changed "Become a Fan" buttons on brand pages to "Like" buttons. In making this change, Facebok stated that administrators of brand pages will still be able to call the people connected to their page "fans."

"fans" and respond to any posts by prospects and customers. It's important to create a dialog with your followers, rather than just have a running monologue of business information.

LinkedIn Basics for Marketing Services Providers

LinkedIn has always been a business-oriented social networking site. So it's a natural place to set up shop and create a presence in order to connect with other businesses. It helps you to keep in touch with colleagues and customers, find experts, or show off your own expertise. LinkedIn allows you to interact and network with other professionals from around the globe. So where do you start?

Begin by building your profile; make sure it is complete. You want to put your best foot forward and further your brand. So upload that logo, and in the Summary and Specialties section, remember to use plenty of keywords to make your business searchable.

> ***TIP: Check out the LinkedIn profiles of individuals and companies you respect as a model for your own.***

Once your profile is ready to go, it's time to make connections. You have several different options to grow your network. First, you can use webmail import to see who is already in your email contact list that is already on LinkedIn. You can also upload your contacts from Outlook, Palm, ACT! and Mac Address. Then you can search for any companies you currently do business with or have had contact with in the past to see if they have a LinkedIn profile. Once you get connected, you can look at that person/company and their connections and gain introductions in order to widen your network. You can also send out invite emails to anyone you can't find on LinkedIn, but would like to connect with. LinkedIn will also suggest other users you may wish to link to. Be sure to peruse that list periodically to see who else may have joined. Remember, every time you link to someone it expands your network not by one, but by however many first degree connections that person has!

Once you have your profile set up and some connections are made, look through your connections to see if there are any customers you could ask to give you a recommendation. This is basically a testimonial that will show up on your LinkedIn page. You should examine who you are connected to that could benefit from a recommendation from you. Don't hesitate to start the ball rolling and spread the testimonial love by leaving positive feedback on the recommendation form for your connections.

Become a joiner by checking out LinkedIn Groups. You can search using keywords to find some groups where you can exchange ideas with colleagues or establish your expertise with your target market. Pick a few and prepare to be active, posting news articles or inserting yourself into the middle of an online discussion.

You can also build credibility and display your business know-how by answering questions. Browse the "Answers" section where you can post a thought-provoking question or find a question that you know the answer to. You can check out the various categories, or use the advanced search feature to drill down for more specific categories of questions.

You'll also want to visit the LinkedIn Applications page where you can look at the optional add-ons that can spice up your LinkedIn experience. You can add a reading list to show viewers books you suggest. Or you can embed a presentation. You can even sync your WordPress blog posts to your profile. Adding an application or three can definitely make your business stand out and draw more attention, so take some time to pick out a few that will really complement your LinkedIn profile.

To get the most out of your LinkedIn experience, make sure you log in, update your status and interact with your connections at least two to three times a week. You want to make sure your presence is obvious. If you never log in and engage others, answer or post questions or update your profile status, then you'll be missing out on the benefits of social media for your business.

URL-Shortening

One facet of many social media sites that marketers are forced to account for is the character-limit on the corresponding site. For example, Twitter only allows you to enter 140 characters.

To account for this, marketers are required to ensure that their messages only contain important words and phrases. But one more way to handle these limitations is to shorten URLs that you may include in your posts.

interlinkONE has built a tool—ilink.me—to help people do this. You can use it for free at http://www.ilink.me

URL-shortener tools like ilnk.me, bit.ly, tinyURL and others are easy to use. They can dramatically reduce the amount of characters in the URL that you are looking to share with others. But along with shortening the URL, these tools can also provide another great benefit: they enable you to track how many people are clicking on your links!

For example, let's say that you want to share a white paper with your social media fans, friends, and followers. The PDF of the white paper may exist on a web server, with a URL such as http://www.MyCompany.com/Resources/WhitePapers/SavingMoneyToday.pdf

If you place that in a URL-shortening tool, the resulting URL may be something like http://ilnk.me/75612.

If you were to then post an entry on Twitter, such as "Check out our new white paper for tips on saving money at http://ilnk.me/75612," your URL-shortening tool would allow you to see how many people clicked the link from Twitter.

You could then create another short URL for that same white paper, and post that one on Facebook. You would receive a whole new set of reports for that URL, and that target audience.

Tactics like this can help you to compare how effectively certain social media sites are working for you.

Building a Social Media Plan

Like anything in business or marketing, you have better success if you have a plan in place. Strategy before tactics is worth repeating here. Your marketing plan needs an online marketing plan to include social media. This should not be left up to Barbara the receptionist who is good at Facebook ☺.

This checklist will guide you in making your social media experience successful and can be the basis for building your social media plan. It makes mention of a few sites we haven't discussed, so be sure to check them out.

☐   Actions are below for social media execution.

- o   A company representative should be active on two to four different social media sites on a daily/weekly basis in order to connect with others and build relationships.
    - LinkedIn
    - Twitter
    - Facebook
    - YouTube
    - Scribd
    - Xing
    - Flickr
- o   Items to post:
    - Behind the scenes pictures
    - Client success stories
    - Testimonials
    - Press releases
    - How-to videos
    - Articles
    - Podcasts
    - Answers to frequently asked questions
    - Questions (to invite answers/comments from others)
    - Company announcements & upcoming events & specials
    - Tips to help your prospects and clients
    - Contests & giveaways

- ☐ *Want to look at a huge list of social media sites by category? You might be able to find a couple of sites where your prospects hang out…a good place for you to network! Check out:* http://ilnk.me/SocialWeb

Figure 22. Having a Plan Helps You Get Noticed

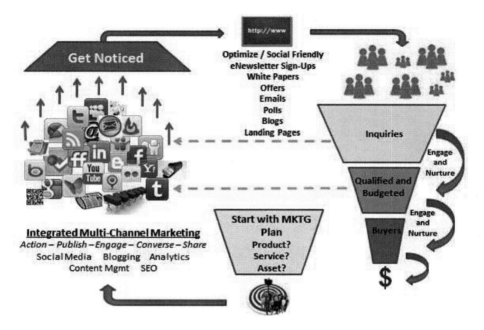

Figure 22 demonstrates why social media activities will only succeed with a plan --- there are so many channels, but when used properly, they can lead to new sales.

TIP: *The idea is to get noticed. Pull them in, drive them into your web site and give them ways to interact and engage!*

Now is the Time!

There is a great deal to digest in this chapter, especially if you have not yet started using social media, personally or professionally, on a regular basis. Don't be intimidated. It is easier than it may sound. But also, don't put off this important step. If you are not already talking to customers about social media services, start learning how to do so now by personally participating. Once you get your feet wet, I have no doubt that you and your staff will have many, many great ideas about how to use social media for your own business purposes, as well as how to leverage this emerging world of communications for the benefit of your customers.

So far in this book, we have been talking about the past and present. Now let's turn our attention to the future of our businesses.

Keys to Success

- There are unwritten rules of social media etiquette; educate yourself.

- Many marketers struggle with how to monetize their social media presence. Perhaps how to monetize is the wrong question to be asking. Rather, it is a part of the overall communications strategy of any successful company today.

- Social media sites help to further your brand, increase visibility, encourage web site traffic, improve customer service and more.

- It is important to start with a small number of sites where you can easily maintain a presence.

- There are three top social media sites that most benefit your marketing services provider business—Twitter, Facebook and LinkedIn.

- A blog is a web site that is generally maintained by an individual with regular entries of commentary, descriptions of events or other material such as graphics or videos. Blogs are an excellent means of getting a discussion going.

- Twitter is an excellent micro-blogging platform for spreading the word about company news, special events, discounts and more.

- Keep in mind that Twitter is a conversational tool, not a one-way onslaught of promotional tweets.

- Did you know that Facebook has over 500 million users? Don't you think your current and future customers are among them?

- Post a Facebook badge or widget on your website to let your site visitors know about your Facebook page.

- LinkedIn allows you to interact and network with other professionals from across the globe.

- Once you have your LinkedIn profile set up and some connections are made, look through your connections to see if there are any customers whom you could ask to give you a recommendation.

- Become a joiner by checking out LinkedIn Groups.

- To get the most out of your LinkedIn experience, make sure you log in, update your status and interact with your connections at least two to three times a week.

- Placing your business profile on Twitter and sending out tweets is just the tip of the iceberg; there are many useful applications that have been developed for Twitter users.

- Don't be intimidated. Working in the world of social media is easier than it may sound. But also, don't put off this important step.

CHAPTER TEN

MARKETING SERVICES PROVIDERS— THE FUTURE

Where the Path Will Take Us

Remember that making the transformation from a mailing/fulfillment operation to a marketing services provider is not a one-time effort, but rather it is a journey down an ever-evolving road. This means that building a lasting business isn't all about what's going on today. Making the transformation to a marketing services provider requires looking forward to the future and anticipating (okay, trying to anticipate) the changes ahead. This includes changes in technology, changes in services, and changes in needs…you get the idea.

While we may not have a crystal ball and a head turban like the old Johnny Carson routine with Carnac the Magnificent, there are a few things that we already know are coming in the near or not-so-distant future that will have an impact on your business …

In the near future, expect an increasing number of marketing services providers to handle the majority of a company's most urgent marketing needs. Printing, mailing and fulfillment will still be involved – largely with personalized or customized/versioned printed and non-printed materials. But marketing services providers will also be managing and executing email efforts. They will help their clients optimize social media. They will deploy campaigns using QR codes, mobile marketing channels and other new marketing technology. They will provide marketing dashboards that allow their marketing clients to not only monitor campaign results, but to easily set up and change campaigns with an easy-to-use tool set in a self-service model.

As time and technology marches on, there will be more ways for people to go online and more ways to respond to a campaign offer. The channels will truly be multiplying and diversifying. Proactive, innovative and successful marketing services providers will stay on top of all this without skipping a beat. They will harness the technology with the necessary tools; and while the technology will evolve, the fundamentals of marketing will remain the same.

You may also anticipate that the marketing services providers of the future will be more involved with the creative on the front end of the campaigns, becoming a single-source business – acting as marketing agency, printer, mailer, fulfillment house and analytics manager. We've mentioned the whole "one-stop shop" idea a few times now, and that's exactly where the marketing services provider model is headed, expanding as technology and clients' needs require.

One thing is certain: the run lengths, turn times and overall volumes of printing will continue to decline. The volumes of hardcopy mail will also continue to decline. While there are opportunities for enterprising operations to grab more market share of a declining market, even many of those businesses are adding marketing services to stimulate growth and to be that one-stop shop for micro businesses.

Staying in the Loop

The best way to stay on top of technology is to use it. I purchased an Apple iPad not too long after they first came out. I wasn't convinced I needed one. But I knew I needed to understand the attraction of this tablet computing device that is selling more than a million units a month. Of course, I also have my iPhone. I am now addicted to both and am finding more and more uses for them. In fact, I upgraded to the iPad2 when it came out. It also helps me understand what my customers are doing with these devices, why they are important to them and how I can leverage those technologies in my own business.

I'm not saying that you should buy every new gadget that comes out. But you should certainly acquire and use technology that you see starting to ramp up. Talk to your customers about what they are using and why. Subscribe to technology newsletters such as *Technology Review, IT World, InfoWorld, PC World* and *Forbes.* Most of these publications have a number of topics to choose from and deliver customized newsletters to your email box on a daily or weekly basis. CNET.com is also another good source of technology information, as is TechCrunch. You can also safely download many software applications from CNET, many of which are free.

Here are some more ideas to get you going:

- Set up Google Alerts using keywords that will let you know when something new is happening in your areas of interest or with your key customers and prospects. Keep those keywords updated as you learn about new things.

- Subscribe to RSS feeds from various news outlets and blogs, such as Tamar Weinberg's Techipedia or one or more of the WhatTheyThink blogs. Google Reader is a good interface for putting these feeds into one location.

- Do you have a smart phone? If not, acquire one, and make sure it has a QR Code reader or download one into the phone. Then snap a few QR Codes to familiarize yourself with this technology.

- Read Mashable.com Daily
- Research and understand augmented reality
- Join and attend conferences that specifically focus on marketing – mobile, social media, and more

Working Together

Writing this book has been an amazing experience for me. I hope you have enjoyed reading it as much as I enjoyed producing it. But in today's virtual and digital world, and in light of the journey I hope you are undertaking, our experience together doesn't end with reading the book.

As I have referenced several times, the book has a resource site on the web at http://www.NewPathToProfit.com. It contains many tools and lots of additional information that we will keep updated on a regular basis. It also offers the opportunity for you to participate in discussions with your peers who have also read the book, as well as our experts.

Join us. Let's move into the future together!

Keys to Success

- Making the transformation to a marketing services provider requires looking forward to the future and anticipating (okay, trying to anticipate) the changes ahead.

- In the near future, expect an increasing number of marketing services providers to handle the majority of a company's most urgent marketing needs. Print/mail/fulfillment will still be involved.

- As time and technology marches on, there will be more ways for people to go online and more ways to respond to a campaign offer. The channels will truly be multiplying and diversifying.

- You may also anticipate that the marketing services providers of the future will be more involved with the creative on the front end of the campaigns, becoming a single-source business – acting as marketing agency, printer, mailer, fulfillment service and analytics manager.

- The best way to stay on top of technology is to use it.

- We are starting to see some mailing/fulfillment firms and suppliers launch apps for the iPad/iPhone. What about you?

- You don't have to buy every new gadget that comes out. But you should certainly acquire and use technology that you see starting to ramp up.

APPENDICES

Appendix A: Business Plan

Table of Contents

Appendix B: Marketing Plan: Putting Marketing into Action

A sample marketing plan that has been completed can be located in the online resource page for this book.

Company Name: Print Co	My Name:
Address: xxx	Website: Printcompany.com
City/State/Zip: xx, WA	Updated last:

What does my company do? : Provide Marketing and Print services

My Email:
Today's Date: …
My Marketing Budget:

Target Market: SMB and Enterprise Marketing departments that need additional resources to execute their marketing strategy To be a partner of these companies to help them better market their products and services.

The 4 P's of Marketing

Product or Service:
Marketing and Print services

Price:

Placement:
Getting the product to the customer
Distribution Channels – Direct / indirect
Verticals: - Telecom, Automobile, Healthcare, Financial Services
Inventory
Warehouse Management
US Footprint

Hosted web site will host electronic content

Promotion:

Promotional Strategy
Target   Audience,   Channels?   Media   Types?   Response
Mechanisms
Advertising
Sales Promotion
PR and Publicity
MarCom Budget
Direct Mail, Website, Conferences, Magazines, Online Banner Ads

Goals and Objectives:

Bring in 2 new local businesses every month

Value/Propositions:

Be able to bring in more customers, retain and grow existing customers, track results, promote effectively

How are they aligned to the business need of the prospect?

If the customer is able to track the results of their campaigns they'll be able to determine which media types bring in the best leads. With these leads they can grab a prospect's information, and follow up on them while targeting their own personal interests, making the campaign even more effective. All this should result in bringing in more customers.

My Competitors:

My Company Strengths:

Great customer service, Local, Quick turnaround time

My company weaknesses:

Everyone thinks of us as just a mail house

My Marketing Execution Plan for [Year]:

- Send out hard copy e-newsletter every quarter

- Campaign to collect emails for enewsletter signup
- Enewsletter 1 pager sent every month (need a writer)
- Postcard with pURL every other month to verticals with A/B testing
- Whitepaper inclusion 2 a year
- Blog Posts
- Case Studies (customer short story – placed in inventory, blog post and web site)
- Thought leader one pagers "the Printer one to one"
- Run Holiday promotions (July and Dec)
- Reach out to various magazines where your prospects are
- Social Media outreach LinkedIn, Twitter, Facebook
- You tube videos of case studies (customer testimonial)
- Host a seminar

Jan	1	2	3	Jul	1	2	3
Feb	1	2	3	Aug	1	2	3
Mar	1	2	3	Sep	1	2	3
Apr	1	2	3	Oct	1	2	3
May	1	2	3	Nov	1	2	3
Jun	1	2	3	Dec	1	2	3

Future Plans to Keep In Mind:

- X
- Y

Appendix C: Detailed Marketing Campaign Questionnaire

1) Purpose/ Goal of Campaign:
a) Purpose:
[ ] event
[ ] Product Launch
[ ] Promotion/offer

b) # of People being targeted:
c) # of contact databases
d) Message you would like to convey:

_____

_____

_____

2) What creative tools do you require for this campaign? :
[ ] Direct Mailer
[ ] Landing Page
[ ] Email Blast
[ ] Promotional Hand Out / Offer

_____

_____

_____

3) Name of Campaign/Event:

_____

_____

_____

4) Date of Event:

_____

_____

_____

Direct Mailer

(Please remember to specify what you would like variable/personalized on this card and if it requires a personalized Landing Page. Anything personalized generally requires a contact list in the form of an Excel or Access file.)

1) Dimensions of mailer:

_____

_____

_____

2) Front Description:
a) Headline: _____

_____

b) Text: _____

_____

_____

3) Back Description:
a) Headline: _____

_____

b) Text_____

_____

_____

4) Are we printing for you?

_____

_____

_____

5) If not please specify a printer:

_____

Landing Page:

1) Landing Page Address (if personalized):

a) (Please supply multiple suggestions in the case that your first idea is already owned. Example format *www.campaign/* first&lastname.*com* or *www.first&lastname.campaign.com*)

_____

_____

_____

_____

_____

_____

_____

2) Is your page personalized?

_____
_____
_____

3) Are there any logos you require for the site? :

_____
_____
_____

4) Text (Main Message):

_____
_____
_____
_____
_____
_____

5) Contact information required for input or verification
(Email, Cell number, etc.)

_____
_____
_____

6) Questions and Response Options
a) Question 1:_____

_____
_____
_____

b) Response 1: (single/multiple/open ended) _____

_____
_____
_____

a) Question 2:_____

_____
_____
_____

b) Response 2: (single/multiple/open ended) _____

_____

_____

_____

_____

a) Question 3:_____

_____

_____

b) Response 3: (single/multiple/open ended) _____

_____

_____

_____

a) Question 4:_____

_____

_____

_____

b) Response 4: (single/multiple/open ended) _____

_____

_____

_____

a) Question 5:_____

_____

_____

_____

b) Response 5: (single/multiple/open ended) _____

_____

_____

_____

Email Blast:

1) Ready Date:

_____

_____

_____

_____

_____

2) Launch Date:

_____

_____

_____

3) Is your email personalized? :

_____

_____

_____

4) Are there any logos you require for email? :

_____

_____

_____

5) Text:

_____

_____

_____

_____

Promotional Hand Out/Offer:

1) Ready Date:

_____

_____

_____

2) Launch Date:

_____

_____

_____

3) What are you offering? :

_____

_____

_____

4) Does it require a landing page? :

_____

_____

5) Do these hand outs require access/password codes for the customer to receive their gift?

_____

_____

_____

Appendix D: Staying in Touch with Marketers

Associations/Events

The DMA (Association and Events)	http://www.the-dma.org
Marketing Profs (Online Association)	http://www.marketingprofs.com/
Mobile Marketing Association	www.mmaglobal.com/
CMO Council	http://www.cmocouncil.org/
American Marketing Association	http://www.marketingpower.com
Business Marketing Association	http://www.marketing.org
Ad:tech	http://www.ad-tech.com/
Inbound Marketing Summit	http://inboundmarketingsummit.com/
SES Conference & Expo	http://www.searchenginestrategies.com/
Online Marketing Summit	http://www.onlinemarketingsummit.com/
SXSW	http://2008.sxsw.com/interactive/
MFSA	http://www.mfsanet.org/
NAPL	http://www.napl.org/

Marketing Resources

Mashable.com	http://mashable.com/
Mobile Marketing	http://www.mobilemarketer.com/

More Marketing Resources available in the online resource page for this book …

Publications (Online and Print)

B to B Magazine (online)	http://www.btobonline.com/
DMNews	http://www.dmnews.com/
Advertising Age	http://www.adage.com

More Marketing Publications available in the online resource page for this book…

Appendix E: Marketing Job Description

To successfully offer and execute marketing services, companies may need to invest resources into finding the right employee(s). Scan the QR Code below to access marketing job descriptions that may help in sourcing the right person. We will seek to spell out the type of skills and experience the right candidate should have.

Appendix F: Organizational Charts

These functional organizational charts depict the differences between organizational strategies for maileres and marketing services providers.

Small Lettershop

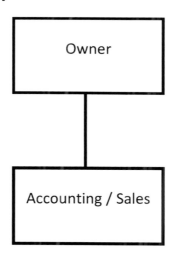

Mid-Sized Mail House

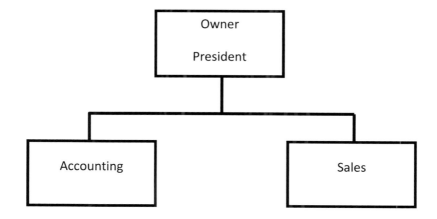

Mid-Sized Mailer/Fulfillment Operation

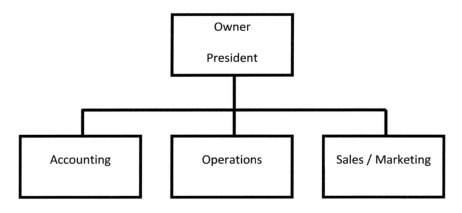

Marketing Services Provider

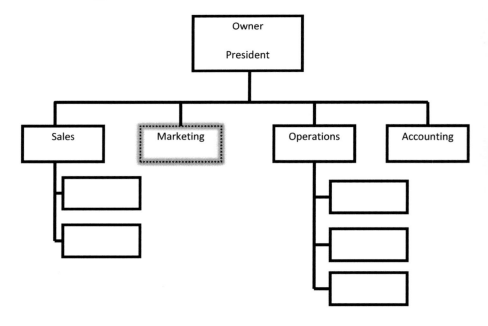

Appendix H: Recommended Reading

The New Community Rules	Tamar Weinberg
Good to Great	Jim Collins
Trust Agents	Chris Brogan
A Whole New Mind	Daniel Pink
The New Rules of Marketing and PR	David Meerman Scott
Marketing Management	Kevin Lane Keller and Philip Kotler
Disrupting the Future	Dr. Joe Webb and Richard Romano
The Mirror Test	Jeffrey Hayzlett
The Chaos Scenario	Bob Garfield
The Power of Direct Marketing: ROI, Sales, Expenditures and Employment in the U.S.	Direct Marketing Association (www.the-dma.org)
Who Moved My Cheese	Spencer Johnson, M.D.
Bit Literacy	Mark Hurst
Getting Business: Opportunities for Commercial Printers and Their Clients in the New Communications Arena	Dr. Joe Webb and Richard M. Romano

GLOSSARY

Scan the QR Code below to access the most recent Glossary of terms from this book.

As the worlds of marketing and communications continue to shift, we will update the Glossary to keep you up-to-date!